# Powerful Wisdom

# Powerful Wisdom

*Voices of Distinguished
Women Psychotherapists*

Lourene A. Nevels
Judith M. Coché

Jossey-Bass Publishers · San Francisco

Substantial discounts on bulk quantities of Jossey-Bass books are available to corporations, professional associations, and other organizations. For details and discount information, contact the special sales department at Jossey-Bass Inc., Publishers. (415) 433-1740; Fax (415) 433-0499.

For sales outside the United States, contact Maxwell Macmillan International Publishing Group, 866 Third Avenue, New York, New York 10022.

Manufactured in the United States of America

The paper used in this book is acid-free and meets the State of California requirements for recycled paper (50 percent recycled waste, including 10 percent postconsumer waste), which are the strictest guidelines for recycled paper currently in use in the United States.

The ink in this book is either soy- or vegetable-based and during the printing process emits fewer than half the volatile organic compounds (VOCs) emitted by petroleum-based ink.

**Library of Congress Cataloging-in-Publication Data**

Nevels, Lourene A., date.
    Powerful wisdom : voices of distinguished women psychotherapists / Lourene A. Nevels, Judith M. Coché. — 1st ed.
       p.    cm. — (the Jossey-Bass social and behavioral science series)
    Includes bibliographical references and index.
    ISBN 1-55542-570-4
    1. Women psychotherapists.  2. Women psychotherapists—Vocational guidance.  I. Coché, Judith.  II. Title.  III. Series.
RC440.82.N48  1993
616.89'14'082—dc20
                93-3621
                CIP

FIRST EDITION
*HB Printing*   10  9  8  7  6  5  4  3  2  1           *Code 9364*

The Jossey-Bass
Social and Behavioral Science Series

For my husband, Jim
— *Lourene A. Nevels*


I dedicate these pages to the wellsprings of powerful wisdom in each of us, male and female. Especially, I remember twenty-five years of collaboration on the power of female psychologists with my late husband, Erich. These years together germinated work to follow.
— *Judith M. Coché*

# Contents

The First Generation • The Feminization of the Profession • The Development of Empathy • Early Training Through Socialization • Effects of Gender on Therapy Outcome • The "Woman as Therapist" Questionnaire • Who Speaks with These Voices? • The Profiles in the Chapters • The Humble Pioneer—Rachel Cox • Gender and Psychotherapy • Woman as Therapist

What Traditional Theories Lack • Growth Through Connection • An Ethic of Responsibility and Care

# List of Tables

# *Preface*

*Powerful Wisdom* tells the stories of women psychotherapists who have achieved distinction in the last half of the twentieth century. It offers a window into the world of female psychologists and family psychotherapists and traces how they have become skilled and successful through a combination of personal and professional pathways. It also offers an in-depth exploration of the inner world of the woman practitioner. Nearly two hundred senior female psychologists and family therapists volunteered information through our questionnaire, "Woman as Therapist," and this has allowed us to identify the themes we explore in this book.

## The Need for This Book

The related fields of social work, clinical nursing, professional psychology, and psychiatry increasingly train females as direct service providers. Recent theoretical work in the fields of adult female development and feminist family therapy stresses the necessity of a specific knowledge base for understanding female adult life stages, especially regarding career development. *Powerful*

*Wisdom* attempts to integrate a selected body of theory in adult development with information gathered through written interviews. It provides valuable information about the career—and the person—of the accomplished female mental health professional. To our knowledge, this has not been done to date. *Powerful Wisdom* may be unique in presenting the experience of distinguished women who have flourished in careers despite many obstacles, including gender discrimination, minimal mentoring, and nonsupportive parenting.

*Powerful Wisdom* educates the reader about the nature of a career in the mental health professions for women. It also helps the reader to understand and to appreciate women's capacity for personal and professional relationship skills. It is a thorough study of the world of the female mental health professional, written by two women mental health professionals who act as organizers and spokeswomen for the almost two hundred women represented in these pages.

We believe that *Powerful Wisdom* addresses a need. Male and female colleagues tell us that they are interested in this book because there are so few sources of information that have been collected and organized in a similar fashion. We hope this book will be a useful road map for younger female colleagues and that it will provide validation and insight for senior female colleagues who have invested a lifetime of personal and professional energy in facilitating human growth and change.

## Audience

When we began collecting information for *Powerful Wisdom,* we expected the book to be primarily of interest to senior clinicians in our field and to historians in the fields of psychotherapy, family therapy, and applied psychology. We also expected psychotherapists-in-training and people considering psychotherapy as a profession to find the book helpful. However, we were surprised to find that the book was also of interest to people outside the field, especially to clients in psychotherapy, our colleagues in academic settings, and women pursuing various careers and professions.

Because of the level of seniority of many of the respondents to the questionnaire, *Powerful Wisdom* is an informal history of psychotherapy from the vantage point of the female psychotherapist. For this reason, *Powerful Wisdom* can serve as an additional text in courses on the history of psychotherapy and in courses on women's issues. We expect faculty and supervisors in the mental health professions to consider this book for university and training courses in counseling, psychotherapy, and related issues. Because of the section on mentoring and supervision, *Powerful Wisdom* is suitable as a text on supervision and professional issues in the fields of psychology, social work, clinical nursing, psychiatry, family psychotherapy, and women's studies.

Psychotherapy has become a very useful tool for people from all walks of life and at all levels of sophistication. Since there is something a bit mystical about the psychotherapy process for most clients, many would like to learn more about how this process works and more about the world of their own therapists. *Powerful Wisdom* provides this insight.

Because the book deals with issues important for all female professionals, the sections on identity development, the development of professionalism for females, and the influence of gender on self-esteem are useful for people in professions other than the mental health sciences. In this respect, *Powerful Wisdom* is a report of the development of women in a given profession — psychotherapy — that can be generalized to other fields as well.

## Overview of the Contents

*Powerful Wisdom* progresses from a general and theoretical examination of the crucial issues for female adult development, through direct responses from the women represented in our questionnaire, to an examination of future issues and directions.

Chapter One examines the attractiveness of the mental

health professions for women and describes those developmental concerns that predispose women to be effective therapists. The chapter does not argue that women make better therapists. Instead it discusses those factors in female development that are advantageous in this field. Chapter One also describes the characteristics of the women in our sample and paints a picture for the reader of the woman who chooses a mental health profession and achieves success in it.

Chapter Two traces recent research in the theory of adult female development as it applies to the responses of the women in our sample. Recent developments indicate that women have unique ways of learning and knowing, that they have been socialized in predictable ways, and that they conceptualize reality through an emphasis on interpersonal relationships. With special attention to the works of Gilligan, Miller, Josselson, and Belenky, Chapter Two provides a theoretical framework for the women's responses, which we highlight in Chapters Three through Six.

In Chapter Three, we examine successful therapy, using our questionnaire responses. We identify empathy as a crucial ingredient in effective psychotherapy and describe nine other variables that emerged as key. A brief review of research results on the effectiveness of psychotherapy provides a context for understanding our questionnaire data.

Chapter Four reports on the intricacies involved in fulfilling the multiple roles of a personal and professional life. It addresses the necessity of setting priorities in time management and discusses a frequently reported danger, namely, that the intimacy involved in psychotherapy taxes the psychotherapist's energy, resulting in less intimacy at home.

Chapter Five examines our respondents' experiences of gender discrimination, financial discrimination, and sexual harassment. Confronting the obstacles in the high-powered and competitive world of professional psychotherapy and dealing with the inevitable struggles and disappointments make up the body of this chapter. We also identify the qualities and skills — and the coping strategies — our sample has found useful.

In Chapter Six, we look at mentoring and argue that successful career development is often determined in part by the quality of mentoring an individual receives. The mental health professions and academic institutions historically have been male dominated; it is no surprise that women in our sample report having to make their own way with minimal mentoring by either men or women. Our experts stress the need for more female role models and discuss what was helpful — and not so helpful — about their own mentoring experiences.

Chapter Seven reviews and integrates the major themes of the book. Using the data from the "Woman as Therapist" questionnaire (included as the Appendix), we draw conclusions about the fit between female socialization and a career in psychotherapy. We offer an inside view of the adult female mental health professional who chooses to work in direct therapeutic services and is successful in this endeavor. We also offer suggestions for women as they climb this career ladder.

## What This Book Is Not

In reviewing relevant theories on adult female development, we were impressed by how much the field has expanded in the last ten years. For this reason, it was impossible to include valuable theoretical contributions from a large number of sources. We chose to concentrate on major theoreticians and are aware that we overlooked a great number of issues that are both relevant and important. For example, we did not review the feminist family psychotherapy literature because we are discussing the person of the female clinician rather than the practice of psychotherapy.

*Powerful Wisdom* is not a statement against men. The value of men in the lives of the women in these pages is obvious. Men have been central to our own development. We are open in our appreciation of men who have helped us in our own careers. This book is also not a balanced study about men and women in the mental health field. Although we very much respect our male colleagues, it seems to us time to study women in the field; our approach allowed us to do this in greater depth than would have been possible if we had included both genders. A natural follow-up to this book is either a more rigorous research study or a similarly descriptive look at the men in the field.

*Powerful Wisdom* is not a strict experimental research study. It was never intended as such, and we do not attempt to report it as such. Clinicians interested in doing more rigorous research on career development in the mental health professions would set up a study in a very different manner and would use tighter controls in collecting and reporting the data. Nevertheless, we believe that the quotations and anecdotes gathered through our questionnaire are highly informative and representative.

## A Book for the People

Book creation is similar to the process of human conception, birth, and skillful parenting. As all of us who have been parents know, deep satisfaction results from enabling a child to enter the world and from assisting her to make her own place. That child belongs more to the world she inhabits than to the parents who raised her. Similarly, the process of designing and executing the interviews for *Powerful Wisdom* has been a creative, surprising, sometimes joyful, and sometimes frustrating experience. The synergy between the two of us as coauthors has been enriching. The outstanding women who responded warmly to our request for information validate our belief that our field contains women of great stature.

We began this book in 1987 and had planned to publish it in 1990. The tragic illness and death of Erich Coché at age forty-nine slowed the completion of our work. Rather than have Lourene continue as a single author, we changed the schedule and rearranged the authorship. We did not plan to cancel the project because we wanted to share the experiences and words of our respondents. As a result of the same kind of determination described over and over again in these pages, the powerful wisdom of the therapists in our sample is now our gift to present, past, and future female colleagues as well as other interested readers. Although we have organized the information, the women who responded to the interviews actually are the authors of the book.

## Acknowledgments

Despite the old-fashioned notion that a hero is a lone pillar of strength who manages great challenges all by himself, we believe that any successful undertaking requires tremendous personal and professional support from many, many people. This project began in 1987 and took five years to complete. In those five years, a number of individuals stand out as consistently helping us in the data collection process and in the writing of the final text.

Beverly Cutler reviewed and summarized the literature on adult female development. She read various drafts of our chapters, provided research assistance and encouragement, and brainstormed with us on the title for the book. Eileen Glinski typed and retyped all the pages of the manuscript with painstaking attention to detail. We are indebted to her for her efforts. The staff at the offices of Coché and Coché helped organize appointments and mountains of paper and made phone calls to psychotherapists all over the country. Because we believe that a book needs to be read by a variety of people in order to work out the kinks, we wish to thank everyone from Joan Abrams, who has an M.B.A. degree from Harvard University, to Dale Tyson, a Merrill-Lynch financial consultant, to James Nevels, Lourene's husband and an independent entrepreneur, to Stephanie Hughes, a Ph.D. candidate in international business, to Zachary von Menchhofen, a promising opera student who helped at the last minute. It is not always pleasant to receive frank criticism, but it is certainly helpful. *Powerful Wisdom* is richer for all of their efforts.

Lourene's parents, Harold and Idamae Dellinger, are seventy-six years old as this book is published. Lourene is grateful for their example of encouraging growth through letting go and trusting that the foundation they laid would provide support for a lifetime. It is a model of caring that Lourene has used in her own encouragement of others' growth. James Nevels provided both business and legal advisement, made sure questionnaires got printed and mailed, and soothed his wife's occasional frustration by lending a sympathetic ear and sense of humor. He has been an untiring cheerleader throughout Lourene's career as a psychologist.

Juliette Laura Coché is fourteen at the time of this publication. Although her father's death was still fresh in her mind, Juliette granted hours and hours of time to her mom as she worked on this project, including early in the morning, the middle of the night, and on weekends. Juliette is certain that her mother will never retire. She seems to enjoy having a mom who works and has been a patient and supportive member of the team that produced *Powerful Wisdom*.

Erich Coché provided great wisdom, support, and enthusiasm in his assistance with statistical analysis, questionnaire development, and clear clinical research–oriented thinking. Erich was very proud of the advances in the field by women and was proud to be a part of it through teaming with Judith. We miss Erich very much and know that he would have been delighted to see this work come to fruition.

The greatest vote of thanks goes to our experts. Their honesty, warmth, poignancy, pain, and sincere comments about themselves, their families, their work, and their careers form the foundations of this book. Just as a soup can only be as good as its ingredients, this book can only be as good as the responses of the women whose words appear herein. For the 192 respondents, a hearty "thank you." We hope you enjoy the results of your efforts.

Special thanks go to the six women we also interviewed so that we could profile them in the chapters. Rachel Cox, Carol Anderson, Emily Visher, Betty Carter, Claudia Bepko, and Lori Gordon are successful and accomplished professionals. We appreciate their time and their willingness to tell us more about themselves.

A final note of thanks goes to the thousands, perhaps millions, of clients who provided our experts with what they know about psychotherapy. To our own clients, graduate students, and supervisees, a similar note of thanks. Without the challenges they brought to us, none of this would have happened.

*June 1993*                                        Lourene A. Nevels
                                                   *Swarthmore, Pennsylvania*

                                                   Judith M. Coché
                                                   *Philadelphia, Pennsylvania*

# The Authors

**Lourene A. Nevels** has been director of the Counseling and Personal Development Center at Saint Joseph's University in Philadelphia since 1985. She teaches courses in the psychology department at the university and has a private practice in Swarthmore, Pennsylvania. She received her B.A. degree (1966) in English from Otterbein College, her M.S. Ed. degree (1974) in learning and development from Bucknell University, and her Ph.D. degree (1981) in counseling psychology from the University of Pennsylvania. She has provided psychotherapy and supervision for women psychotherapists since 1982 and has conducted workshops on mentoring relationships for women.

**Judith M. Coché** is senior group psychotherapy consultant at the Philadelphia Child Guidance Clinic and associate professor of psychology in psychiatry at the Medical School at the University of Pennsylvania. She is also director of Coché and Coché, a clinical psychology practice. She received her B.A. degree (1964) in sociology from Colby College, her M.A. degree (1966) in psychology from Temple University, and her Ph.D. degree (1975) in human development from Bryn Mawr College.

In 1983, she became a member of the American Family Therapy Association and in 1985 received the diplomate in clinical psychology from the American Board of Professional Psychology. She is a fellow of the American Group Psychotherapy Association and currently serves on its board of directors. For the past fifteen years, Coché has centered her work on family therapy, group therapy, and psychotherapy with female psychotherapists. With her late husband, Erich Coché, she coauthored a book, *Couples Group Psychotherapy* (1990), and a videotape, *Techniques in Couples Group Psychotherapy,* which appeared in print three months before his death in 1990.

# Powerful Wisdom

# 1

## A Collective Profile
## of Women Psychotherapists

*I know I have standards of integrity that are more*
*important to me than impressing the gallery.*
— Rachel Cox

Women psychotherapists have much to teach us of life. The pages
that follow were written from the words and thoughts and feelings of 192 distinguished female psychotherapists and family
therapists. Between 1989 and 1990, each woman gave more than
one hour of her time to complete a written interview covering
her professional and personal development. One hundred and
ninety-two women, tops in their profession, wrote of their experiences as mothers, daughters, wives, lovers, sisters, students,
teachers, psychotherapists. Their struggles with gender discrimination, their convictions about what makes them effective psychotherapists, and their opinions about the nature and the power
of relationships are among the topics they covered.

Many of these women are now in their fifties, sixties,
seventies, and eighties. Many are pioneers in the mental health
profession. Their accomplishments fill volumes about the development of professional psychology and family psychotherapy
since 1915. Young women now in their twenties, thirties, and
forties have a rich legacy, as they begin to carve out the future
of their profession. This new generation of clinicians can learn

1

much from the experiences of the women in these pages. More seasoned male and female clinicians may find themselves reflecting on their own rich experiences as they read the words of their colleagues. They too many learn from our experts. The chapters that follow trace personal and professional pathways that led our expert psychotherapists through multifold struggles to their goal of career satisfaction and professional success.

We hope that our readers will be as inspired, as humbled, as outraged, and as tickled as we were by the provocative thoughts, feelings, and visions of these women. These 192 women are among the pioneers who paved the road for their professional daughters.

### The First Generation

Although women's participation in the profession dates from the 1890s when psychology was emerging as a science, their role in the history of psychology has been a "well-kept secret," according to Scarborough and Furumoto (1987, p. 1).

These early pioneers faced considerable discrimination as they were denied access to graduate programs and fellowships. "Despite barriers, women of excellence pursued their careers. By 1920, sixty-two women in America held Ph.D.'s in psychology" (O'Connell and Russo, 1983, p. 12). Antinepotism rules prevented many married women psychologists from getting jobs in the major universities where their husbands were employed. Women psychologists generally taught in women's colleges or worked in applied settings such as schools, hospitals, or guidance centers.

During World War I, women became prominent in the emerging fields of child development, guidance, and mental testing. By 1944, women held 60 percent of the positions in the schools, hospitals, guidance centers, and similar applied settings. "In contrast, 74 percent of the positions in universities and colleges were held by men. The devaluation of women's work was reflected in the salary differential between the sexes, with fully employed women earning about 20–40 percent less than men" (O'Connell and Russo, p. 17). These patterns continue today, with women underrepresented in academe and overrepresented in educational systems and community mental health and family services agencies.

The post–World War II period was marked by a tremendous growth in the clinical areas of psychology, namely, the training of psychotherapists. This is the era during which the vast majority of our experts were beginning their careers. Their stories represent the "modern history" of women psychologists.

## The Feminization of the Profession

In the last quarter of a century, social work, clinical nursing, professional psychology, and psychiatry have trained females as direct service providers in ever-increasing numbers. Women have consistently outnumbered men in social work for decades. The American Psychological Association reports that female psychologists will soon outnumber male psychologists. The number of bachelor's degree candidates with a psychology major dropped by 9,000 between 1976 and 1986. In that same decade, female graduates in the field increased by 870. This means that more and more women are entering a field that is decreasing in overall numbers. On the graduate level, the number of men receiving doctorates in psychology decreased, although the total number of doctorates awarded has not dropped in the past six years. This means that more doctorates in psychology are being awarded to women (Adler, 1991).

How to explain the trend? Why do the mental health professions appear to be losing appeal for men and gaining appeal for women? Perhaps men, previously lured by the appeal of high private-practice income, are becoming disillusioned. Annual incomes in the mental health professions have always been lower than in medicine, law, and business, despite equivalent training years. Furthermore, it is general knowledge that research monies go first and foremost to the natural sciences, the "hard" sciences. Moreover the ethical and legal issues in psychotherapy become more and more complex: malpractice suits and insurance costs increase annually. Insurance companies challenge third-party payments with ever-increasing vigilance.

Solo practitioners have all but disappeared for economic reasons, and group practices are now the norm. In the opinion of many practitioners, group practices pay less to direct service providers than their training warrants.

Despite gender discrimination and lower income than desired, our experts are quite satisfied. Other rewards, such as prestige and autonomy, seem to have provided ample riches. We begin to wonder if our data tell us something deeper, that the practice of psychotherapy is a natural for women. The field promotes the value of relationships and responsibility to others. It provides an arena for women to develop their natural leadership style. Empathy and caretaking, which are taught to females from birth, contribute to successful psychotherapy outcome.

## The Development of Empathy

A consistent refrain from our experts is that being raised female teaches one skills that are therapeutic for others. Traditional qualities considered natural and appropriate for women in our society resemble qualities necessary for an effective therapeutic relationship. The capacity for empathy ranks first. Our experts report that caring about clients is easy because these women have developed the capacity to be intimate, connected, nurturing, and at the same time, insightful and intellectually sound. They allow themselves to make "deep emotional connections" with their clients. As one woman said, they have "a deep well of emotional reserves." Our experts report the "ability to engage with others" and a "special tolerance for others." It is a good combination for doing psychotherapy.

Their words tell us over and over about the value of "empathy," which is "the ability to experience, comprehend and respond to the inner state of another person" (Surrey, 1985, p. 3). The origins of the capacity for empathy are found in the earliest stirrings of the infant's emerging sense of self, as the baby identifies with its central parent. From birth, we are actively interacting with other people. Research on empathy (Eisenberg and Lennon, 1983; Hall, 1987) shows that females are more likely to cry and exhibit distress when observing another's distress and that females are slightly better at interpreting nonverbal emotional cues.

Jean Baker Miller (Jordan and others, 1991) highlights the interactive quality of the relationship between a baby and its caretaker. "The child experiences a sense of comfort only as the other is also comfortable, or, more precisely, only as they are both engaged in an emotional relationship that is moving toward greater well-being" (p. 13). She says these reactions, experienced by all infants, are much more encouraged in girls.

Out of the complex interweaving between mother and child, the child learns to experience a kaleidoscope of feelings toward — and with — other people. When a trusted caretaker accepts the baby's experience and responds to it, the infant's fear and anger become less distressing and overwhelming. Through sharing feelings, the child develops greater comfort with all feeling states. In addition, the child feels empowered as it sees that it can have an effect on the important people in its life.

## Early Training Through Socialization

Both sexes develop an early sense of self from the interpersonal drama that unfolds between themselves and the adult figures in their lives. But children's caretakers seem to unconsciously encourage boys and girls in different ways. Growing up, girls receive greater approval for attending to their parents' feelings. This early attentiveness to feelings and interest in emotional sharing may well be fundamental to later female orientation toward relationships. Jordan (1984) discusses studies that suggest that girls and boys are equally aware of other people's feelings but that girls are more likely to imagine themselves in the other's place. Boys may well be systematically but subtly diverted from their relational abilities in order not to be bound or controlled by mothers' needs. In this way, they may be able to separate more successfully from their mothers (Surrey, 1985).

Centuries of socialization in Western civilization have trained women to be nurturant, passive, emotional. Women are the caretakers of home and family. Women's self-esteem depends on the knowledge that they are enhancing the development of others (Kaplan and Klein, 1985). Socialization as daughters, sisters, wives, and mothers has provided a wealth of female experience about relationships with others. This ease in expressing feelings enables women psychotherapists to model appropriate and optimal expression of feelings. This capacity to say what matters and say it skillfully provides an antidote to the isolation and distrust that impede our capacity, but not our need, for human intimacy.

Western thinking stereotypes women as "intuitive," as being able to know without an awareness of consciously learning. Intuition, or "feeling something to be so," results in part from women's fine-tuned capacity to weave their affective sensitivities with their cognitive abilities. Jeffrey Kottler described intuition as "a form of organized experience that allows effective therapists to access knowledge and find meaningful patterns" (1991, p. 125). Jean Baker Miller (1976) stated that women have developed their intuitive abilities to a greater degree than men because of their learned positions as subordinates and that women have "succeeded" in their inferior position by learning to be hypersensitive to the expectations and needs of those in the dominant position. Food for thought, indeed. Certainly, both male and female psychotherapists utilize this exquisite sensitivity in appropriately timing interventions and developing insights.

## Effects of Gender on Therapy Outcome

Although our experts report that their gender influences their effectiveness as therapists, research on the influence of gender on the process and outcome of psychotherapy provides mixed data. Early studies on patient improvement were sparse and showed no differences based on therapists' gender (Meltzoff and Kornreich, 1970). Orlinsky and Howard (1980) found that moderately and highly experienced female therapists were equally effective, that highly experienced male therapists were as effective as the women therapists, and that moderately experienced male therapists were significantly less effective than the other three groups. Although some male therapists were as effective as their female colleagues, Orlinsky and Howard report that "the women were much more consistent" (p. 27). Despite their caution about drawing conclusions from limited research, Marecek and Johnson (1980) said, "Gender appears to be a strong determinant of the expression of affect in therapy" (p. 88). Women therapists seem to be more aware of clients' feeling states, and they experienced and expressed more feelings in their interactions with clients. Kirshner, Genack, and Hauser (1978) reviewed the psychotherapy research and concluded, "There appears to be a tendency for patients to be more satisfied with female therapists than with male therapists" (p. 160).

In a review of research since 1980, Mintz and O'Neill (1990) state that gender exerts "an influence on how clients react in therapy, perceive the process of therapy, and are reacted to in therapy" (p. 383). Female therapists are more feeling-oriented in their psychotherapeutic interventions and better able to form therapeutic relationships with clients. And clients report greater satisfaction with female psychotherapists (p. 384).

In 1982, Jones and Zoppel interviewed ninety-nine former therapy clients. Both male and female clients agreed that "women therapists formed more effective therapeutic alliances than did male therapists" (p. 259). They defined *therapeutic alliance* as "interest in, acceptance of, and respect for client" (p 267). Although women therapists were warmer and more attentive, clients reported significant improvement with both male and female therapists.

A 1987 study by Jones, Krupnick, and Kerig reported greater patient satisfaction and improvement of symptoms in therapy with female therapists than with male therapists. "There was clearly a greater comfort in the relationship, and women therapists were judged as more accurate in their perception of their patients' emotional states and experience of the therapy relationship" (p. 346).

Alexandra Kaplan (1987) believes that the nature of the client-therapist relationship has been devalued in clinical training. She states that "much more seems to be known about how a therapist can relate poorly than how a therapist can relate well" (p. 13). She agrees with Howard and Orlinsky's findings that the therapeutic relationship, "as exemplified in the reciprocal interpersonal behavior of the participants" (Kaplan, 1987, p. 12), is more important to client improvement than any treatment technique. Earlier we noted Orlinsky and Howard's finding that moderately experienced male therapists were less effective than moderately experienced female therapists. But moderately experienced female therapists were as effective as highly experienced male and female therapists. We wonder if there is something in the female therapist's life experience that gives her an advantage. Kaplan believes that "the greater capacity of the female therapists, especially in their early years of training, is linked to women's relational development pathway" (1987, p. 21). This makes sense to us.

How did women better therapists? Let's ask the question differently. We believe that we need research that explores for whom — and under what circumstances — men and women are effective therapists. What role does gender play? The data present convincing evidence that women psychotherapists possess skills and values in relating to others and that these skills and values enhance their effectiveness and success. However, the data do not state that one gender does more effective psychotherapy than the other.

How did women acquire these skills and values? How have they interwoven influences from socialization, professional training, and life experience to form their identity as women psychotherapists? In the chapters that follow, we will look to our sample to provide answers to these questions, and we will look to the literature to provide a contextual frame for the stories our women tell us.

## The "Woman as Therapist" Questionnaire

In order to learn more about women who are outstanding psychotherapists, we created a written interview. We called it the "Woman as Therapist" questionnaire. It is included in its entirety in Appendix A. In designing the questions, we drew from theoretical as well as experiential resources and used our knowledge of published theories about the career and personal development of women. We also relied on our years of providing psychotherapy and supervision to women psychotherapists to identify the issues these women raised in our work with them.

A pilot study in February 1988 produced twenty-five respondents to the original form of the questionnaire. In October 1988, we piloted a revised questionnaire with fifty female directors of university counseling centers. The final form of the questionnaire reflects the clarification of items used in the two pilot studies. The questionnaire is a lengthy written interview comprised of thirty-three questions. The questions required respondents to reflect on lessons learned as females in their families and in society and to reflect upon the influence of those lessons on their career choice and their self-image as professional caregivers. Respondents described how they thought their relationships with friends, husbands, children, and parents helped or hindered their effectiveness as psychotherapists. They also described the obstacles they overcame and the support received along their journey.

We developed a coding system and operational definitions for all quantifiable data items. We established interrater reliability for the coding system and calculated means and frequency counts for relevant data. In addition to this formal descriptive data analysis, we collected direct quotations from our respondents. The quotations spoke of the issues more articulately than we could have imagined, and we decided to use them in the book. The direct quotations that sprinkle these pages reveal the personal voices of the women in our sample. These are voices of wit and wisdom that contain strong emotions of gratitude, awe, anger, bitterness, contentment, and compassion.

In an accompanying cover letter, we asked our respondents to "take about one hour" to complete the four-page questionnaire. We realized we were sampling a very busy group of women professionals when we received a number of notes saying they did not have time to complete it. One woman wrote apologizing for not being able to participate. "There is no way that I can even spare one hour as I am behind on deadlines for articles, book chapters, and presentations at the present time. I think one important issue that women have to learn is when to say no." She teaches us a lesson through her example of saying no to us in light of pressing demands on her time.

We also realized that we had underestimated the time required when some women sent back an empty questionnaire, on which they wrote that it took too long to figure out the answers to such questions. They reported that they were tempted to write whole pages on many of the questions and that to condense their answers into the inch and a half of space provided was too frustrating. Nonetheless, many of these highly successful and busy women prepared answers even when it meant adding additional pages to the questionnaire. We also received notes from women who did not have time to fill out the questionnaire but offered words of support for and interest in our project.

Some anecdotal comments were not included in the data analysis but are worth mentioning. We received both cheers and jeers about the project itself. Quite a few women wrote comments like "I wish I would have had the benefit of such advice when I was struggling to become a therapist." More than one respondent said, "I wish I had thought of this first." One woman wrote a note saying she decided not to reply to the questionnaire because she did not want to spend the time developing and writing her thoughts only to have them published by someone else.

Our respondents told us of ways we could have improved our questionnaire. Some wanted to address the importance of their personal psychotherapy in their development as psychotherapists. Some wanted questions with less heterosexual bias, asking us to refer to lovers and same-sex living partners rather than husbands. We appreciated their contributions and learned from our omissions.

We received a note from the husband of a diplomate who died a few months before we mailed the questionnaire, saying how much the themes reflected his wife's interests and asking if we could dedicate the project to her memory. We received several notes from retired psychologists who assumed we did not want their responses. Nothing could be farther from the truth — other retirees are represented in our sample. It saddened us that some of the retirees believed their contributions not to be worthy of inclusion. A sizable portion of the diplomates wrote back saying they were not psychotherapists but were employed in research, administration, teaching, and consultation. This factor reduced our return rate but ensured a sizable sample of practicing clinicians.

Research is serendipitous. We started something, only to create something else. We were surprised to find that this research project provided a meaningful experience for the people who received the questionnaire. The questionnaire raised issues for respondents that many had never considered before. Answering the questions produced unexpected self-reflection and fascinating conversation with colleagues and friends. One woman wrote, "I used this questionnaire as basis for discussion in an ongoing study group of female family therapists. We found we could each write a book based on these provocative questions."

## Who Speaks with These Voices?

We identified two populations for inclusion in the research: women who had been awarded the diplomate from the American Board of Professional Psychology (ABPP) and female members of the American Family Therapy Association (AFTA). Our goal was to tap the expertise of the very experienced and expert female psychotherapist. We also wanted our respondents to represent the range of training within the mental health profession, including master's level and doctoral level clinicians in clinical psychology, educational psychology, and social work.

Fewer than 5 percent of all female psychologists are diplomates. To be eligible to be awarded the diplomate, a psychologist must have had a minimum of five years of professional experience beyond the doctorate and must have completed vigorous written and oral examinations on ethics, clinical casework, and diagnosis. She must demonstrate her skills in providing psychotherapy before a group of examiners, themselves recipients of the diplomate. Although the diplomate is variously referred to as the equivalent of being professionally boarded in medicine, on one hand, and as an unnecessary credential, on the other, we knew that diplomates would be among those at the top of their field.

Our sample of family therapists included Ph.D. psychologists, clinical social workers, nurses, and psychiatrists who meet a similarly rigorous standard of specialized training in marriage and family therapy. The American Family Therapy Association (AFTA) is dedicated to the development of its field through

attention to current and emerging issues. Its members are trainers and teachers of family therapy in many countries. Because
of the level of expertise required for membership, a very small
percentage of female family therapists are members of AFTA.

Questionnaires were mailed to all female diplomates (over
four hundred people) and all female members of AFTA (over
three hundred people). The return rate was over 25 percent for
both groups. Our final sample consists of completed questionnaires from 117 diplomates and 75 AFTA members, a total of
192 respondents.

Our respondents ranged in age from thirty-three to eighty-
five at the time they completed the questionnaire. Some had received their highest academic degree many years ago — an average
of 22.5 years to be exact. We were delighted to realize that our
range of respondents was telling us the history of psychotherapy.
One hundred and forty-three of the women held doctoral degrees;
48 held master's degrees, and 1 woman had a bachelor's degree.
Table 1.1 presents a breakdown of academic degrees and dis-
ciplines represented in the sample. Most respondents were currently providing direct service delivery. Only 15 had retired.
Over 56 percent were currently married, 20 percent had never
married, 14.5 percent were divorced, and 9 percent were widowed. Seventy percent were mothers.

Table 1.1. Discipline and Degree of Respondents.

| Discipline | Degree | |
| | Doctorate (75% of respondents) (%) | Master's (25% of respondents) (%) |
| --- | --- | --- |
| Clinical psychology | 45.0 | 8.0 |
| Psychology (unspecified) | 26.0 | 19.0 |
| Social work | — | 45.0 |
| School psychology | 14.5 | — |
| Counseling psychology | 8.5 | 3.0 |
| Human development | 3.0 | 1.0 |
| Family therapy | — | 5.0 |
| Nursing | — | 5.0 |
| Mental health counseling | — | 5.0 |
| Other | 3.0 | 9.0 |

Work settings included private practices (26 percent), universities (19.5 percent), schools (12.6 percent), hospitals (10.7 percent), community mental health (9.3 percent), research centers (8.1 percent), private agencies (6.3 percent), business/industry (2.3 percent). The typical composite respondent is married, has children, holds a doctoral degree, and has two decades of work experience. It seemed to us that these women would have much to tell us. They did.

Many of our interviewees are pioneers and were among very few females in their graduate programs. Many pursued career goals despite family and personal pressure to devote primary energy to home and family. Most respondents are wives and mothers. Their learnings as sisters, daughters, wives, and mothers enhance their skills as effective therapists, but they tell us of role conflicts that involve time shortage and emotional energy drain. However, they report few regrets about their choices. They tell us that their relationships with those they love impact on their self-esteem, sense of well-being, and life decisions. These women report high career satisfaction, despite moderate earning power and lengthy training.

Differences in attitudes and values between diplomates and family therapists turned out to be minimal, although they came to the practice of psychotherapy from different pathways. Most diplomates earned a doctoral degree in clinical psychology while most family therapists had a master's degree in social work. During their graduate training, family therapists were exposed to twice as many female faculty members, supervisors, and fellow students as the diplomates.

Theoretical models of psychotherapy present many options for the trainee. In addition, most clinical psychologists are trained differently from most family therapists. Nevertheless, our two subsamples agreed about the nature of those qualities they considered important in the therapy process. Family therapists rated the belief in human potential highest; diplomates rated empathy highest, but both qualities are more spiritual than intellectual.

Other chapters in this book present information about the personal life choices of our respondents. Family therapists were more likely to be married (63 percent) than diplomates

(53 percent). Of those who married, more family therapists became mothers (80 percent) than diplomates (64 percent). Diplomates in our sample were about five years older on the average
than family therapists. Paradoxically, family therapists reported
greater incompatibility between personal and professional roles
than did the diplomates. In reflecting on this very interesting
finding, we wondered whether it might be related to their stronger
tendency to marry and raise children. Combining multiple
stressful roles year after year would seem to us logically to lead
to incompatibilities. We appreciated their honesty in reporting
this information.

## The Profiles in the Chapters

After the data were analyzed, we selected a representative expert for each chapter. We wanted to relate one woman's story
to the theme of each chapter so that readers could know our
informants personally. We selected respondents who have been
public figures in their profession for some time, whose contributions range from teaching and writing to founding graduate
programs. All were gracious enough to agree to our use of their
names in telling their stories. In a telephone interview in fall
1992, we asked for details that were not included in the questionnaire. These questions concentrated on their work contributions
because each women featured in a chapter seemed important
to us as a model for future professional development.

Each profile brings to life the themes of the chapter in
which it is presented. In this first chapter, we describe a personal interview with Rachel Cox. Eighty-nine years old at the
time of this writing, Rachel's voice is the most senior. Her husband of over fifty years had just died. Age and loss have not
prevented Rachel's remarkable perseverance from being victori-
ous: at the time of the interview she was writing a book about
human development.

## The Humble Pioneer — Rachel Cox

Rachel Cox was born in 1904. When we visited her, she spoke
softly and clearly about three decades of dedication to progress

in mental health. Rachel has been a pioneer in every sense of the word. She has received awards from the Pennsylvania Psychological Association, the Philadelphia Society of Clinical Psychologists, and other organizations for her excellence as a professional psychologist. She has acted as a role model for hundreds of female graduates of the Department of Human Development at Bryn Mawr College, a department that she founded. During the 1960s and 1970s, this department was one of the few training facilities in the Philadelphia area that enabled men and women to work toward a Ph.D. part-time, so that they could integrate academics with their adult lives. It was common for students to spend up to a decade completing a rigorous Ph.D. degree.

We chose to focus on Rachel for two reasons. First, her work has been exemplary in the field of mental health at a time when women in leadership were rare. Second, there is a three generation lineage of mentoring passing from Rachel through Judith to Lourene, the authors of this book. At age nineteen, Judith visited Rachel at her home. This visit was instrumental in Judith's choice to become a psychologist. Rachel said she had had similar interviews with hundreds of young people who came to her home in Swarthmore, Pennsylvania. The year before Rachel retired in 1971, she taught Judith, who was in her first year as a graduate student at Bryn Mawr College. And in 1982, when Judith applied for her diplomate in clinical psychology, Rachel stood by as a reference and support.

Lourene was the director of a university counseling center when she came to Judith to learn group psychotherapy skills. This book developed from that meeting. This three generation lineage from one female mentor to another continues the high standards that Rachel Cox modeled. In her succinct and straightforward fashion she stated, "I don't accept . . . that I am successful. I know I have standards of integrity that are more important to me than impressing the gallery."

In September 1992, Rachel was as petite and as articulate as Judith had long remembered. Rachel looked Judith straight in the eye and said, "Well now, Judy, what do you want from me?" We asked her about her years as a student at the University of Pennsylvania. She smiled. "When I went to Penn, some

of that stuff that happened was just terrible. I was already doing
something that I wanted to know how to do better. I had been
a director of education, and I was already doing some counseling. I had a Master of Arts in English from Columbia University, but I thought that a degree in psychology would help me
to do better work." One of Rachel's classes was a large seminar
in an amphitheater, in which a male professor interviewed "a
little black mother." Rachel was horrified to hear this professor
say, "Madam, your son is an imbecile." The mother replied,
"Sir, you speak very plainly." Rachel's comment: "I thought this
was God-awful."

After she received her Ph.D. in 1943, Rachel straight-
forwardly pursued her life's work. "I decided that if you wanted
to make a difference in kids' lives, you had to start when they
were young, so I decided that I wanted the Lower Merion school
system [in suburban Philadelphia] to start a counseling program
in the elementary schools. They had never done this before. We
started out with a budget of $3,000 per year, including my ser-
vices, and we grew from there. It was about 1946 when I began
this. I had two small children, and I was afraid of damaging
my car. It was war years and we couldn't get replacements. I
wouldn't have known how to get from one place to another."

Katherine McBride, at that time president at Bryn Mawr
College, invited Rachel Cox to lecture half-time. "The teaching gradually grew as I began. We started a counseling service.
We decided to go where the principals wanted us to be. This
seemed like a smart way to proceed. At the Merion School, there
was a child with school phobia. The school superintendent met
with the parents, and they all agreed about the way to handle
it. They said, 'Dr. Cox, just lock the door.' I didn't agree with
this. I was very upset about the way they wanted it handled,
and I couldn't get it out of my mind. The meeting was on Friday. On Saturday, I still couldn't forget about the child while
I was sitting at home and watching a movie. I kept thinking
about it. I never did anything like this before, but I was con-
vinced that we would be making a mistake. I called the school
superintendent at home and said, 'I have doubts about locking
the door on this child. It is not good for this child.' But the school

superintendent told me to just let the counselor go ahead, that it would be all right. So when the counselor got to school that's what she did. The little girl put her fist through the glass door and ran away. People paid more attention to me in the school after that incident." This anecdote illustrates how Rachel eventually was able to make significant changes in the system.

In 1975, Rachel took an "early retirement" (in her words) at age seventy-one to join her husband who had been invited to teach in England. In the thirty years of Rachel's career in the counseling service in the Lower Merion School District, the budget had jumped from $3,000 to $300,000 annually. The services were praised by colleagues and families. Rachel named the counseling department at Bryn Mawr College The Child Study Institute. It included a child guidance clinic that specialized in assessment and counseling. When Rachel Cox retired, she was replaced by three full-time professionals: a department of counseling chair and professor of development, a chair of the Child Study Institute, and a new head of counseling services in the Lower Merion schools. Rachel was sorely missed for years thereafter.

We asked Rachel Cox how her gender had impacted on her career. She told the story of a woman colleague whom she had known some years before, whose political sense was exquisite. "Being a woman made it possible for her to do things she could not have done if she had been a man. She could smooth things over — she would just kind of pick up on the things in a situation that were important to her and figure out how to make things move on to the next step. She had a different perspective from a male, and this was very helpful."

Rachel said that there are two qualities that she believes to be central in the helping process. "The top of the list is to listen. I would tell younger colleagues, 'This is what I have always looked for in students. Don't tell patients and students about your experiences — they don't want to hear that. Just listen to what they have to say and let them work out their own solutions, because that's the only solution that people can use anyway.' Second, I would tell younger colleagues to feel the pain in the hearts of the people that they work with. Empathy, that's what I call it. I would help them to remember that hearts break on the Main Line, regardless of other circumstances in life."

In closing, Rachel wanted to make it perfectly clear that she was very appreciative of men. "I want to give lots of credit to the men in my life — my father, who wanted me to be more than a housewife, and my husband, who gave me lots of encouragement year after year. I miss him terribly." Rachel's husband died at the age of ninety-two in the summer of 1992.

Rachel continued, "But I come from a long line of strong women. After my father died, my mother pulled herself together and began to buy small pieces of property, real estate. She improved them, and she kept getting a little more and then a little more property. She was so smart. She became quite well known for her business acumen."

As we ended the interview, Rachel began to speak about the book that she was currently working on. Her first book, *Youth Into Maturity,* began as a longitudinal study of high-achieving men and women who had attended Swarthmore College, Haverford College, and Bryn Mawr College. Rachel Cox followed these people for ten years. Well into her seventies, Rachel was traveling to interviews with them in Connecticut, New York, Africa (Tunis) — wherever they lived. She is still working on the project and now has data about these people for thirty years after they were college students. The data is a treasure chest in the field of human development. So is Rachel Cox.

### Gender and Psychotherapy

Although this book concentrates on the experiences of the female members of our profession, many of our respondents express appreciation and affection for those men who occupy important positions in their personal and professional lives. Throughout the pages that follow, we will report some of the roles that men have played in the career development of female psychotherapists.

In the four years that we spent developing the questionnaire, distributing it, and discussing the results with anyone who would listen to us, we experienced a notable pattern of misunderstanding about the purpose of the work. Both men and women, but more men, told us that the questions we asked were of importance and wondered why we didn't include men in the sample. Our answer to them was plain and simple: our field needs to know more about the development of women who become distinguished psychotherapists. The focus of this project was to address this issue.

It is logical but mistaken to assume that the exclusion of men represents a bias toward women. It does not. We respect the value and contributions of our male colleagues and hope that someone chooses to study their development in depth.

We do not state that women make better psychotherapists. We simply note that there is a natural interweaving between the way women are socialized and their choice of psychotherapy as a profession.

## Woman as Therapist

The Stone Center for Developmental Services and Studies at Wellesley College presents a statement about the centrality of intimate relationships in issues of female development. "What is central for the developing woman is action within relationship; participating in the kind of relationship which enhances self and others, meaning that is built around mutual empathic attunement" (Kaplan, 1987, p. 18). The exercise of becoming skillful in the relational bond between therapist and client encourages self-growth and self-esteem for both participants. This doubtless provides a key attraction when young women select this career.

The field of psychotherapy is a very competitive one for the men and women who enter it. In reading the chapters that follow, it should become clear that the profession suits our respondents very well. These chapters will explore in more detail what we have gleaned from research, theory, and personal stories about the experiences of women psychotherapists. These are the experiences of women who are courageous and humble, powerful and compassionate, already wise, and still discovering new insights.

# 2

# Women and Relationships: From Theory to Practice

*The reason I work is to enjoy my relationships.*
— Anonymous

We constructed the "Woman as Therapist" questionnaire from our knowledge of the theories about adult female development and of the issues for the women psychotherapists we have treated, supervised, taught, and mentored. Based on this knowledge, many of the questions explored what women experienced in their relationships and how these experiences influenced their identity.

This chapter will focus on useful concepts from the growing body of literature on adult female development and will present the questionnaire results that reveal the effect of our respondents' relationships on their professional identity. We see remarkable consistency between their comments about the centrality of relationships in their lives and what the theories suggest about female development. In many instances, we lack sufficient evidence from our sample to comment on some areas discussed in the theories. For example, we did not develop questions that could enable us to identify at what stage our experts might be, according to theories of moral, cognitive, and career development. However, throughout the chapter we have provided quotations from responses that we believe serve as examples or illustrations of various stages described in these theories.

During the past decade, models of psychological development increasingly emphasized the relational strengths of women. The writings of Carol Gilligan and Jean Baker Miller, along with other theorists such as Ruthellen Josselson and Mary Belenky and her coauthors, have advanced new models of female development and identity based on women's psychological experiences. Their work has helped to represent the female experience missing from traditional theories of psychological development.

Mainstream developmental theorists (such as Freud, Erikson, Perry, and Kohlberg) associate healthy identity with the dominant Western cultural ideals of achievement, individualism, autonomy, mastery, and self-determination. The emphasis of these traditional theories is on the formation of a distinct and separate self through the processes of separation and individuation from others. Thus, the infant separates from the mother, the adolescent separates from the family, and the adult separates from teachers and mentors in adulthood.

Many of these theorists also acknowledged the importance of relationships to the maturing adult identity. According to Rogers, for example, "Deep relationships are positively valued. To achieve a close, intimate, real, fully communicative relationship with another person seems to meet a deep need in every individual" ([1964] 1973, p. 198). Erikson similarly acknowledged the psychological significance of human interconnection by conceptualizing maturation as the individual's "readiness to be driven toward, to be aware of, and to interact with a widening radius of significant individuals and institutions" ([1959] 1973, p. 100). Yet few theorists, including Rogers and Erikson, explained how the self evolves toward this form of intimacy. Instead, their theories accentuated the value of human separateness. As noted by Miller (1981), beyond Erikson's initial stage of psychosocial development, which culminates in the establishment of basic trust, the goal of every other stage until young adulthood involves complex steps of increasing differentiation. Intimacy and generativity, according to Erikson, are possible only after the consolidation of identity.

## What Traditional Theories Lack

Traditional developmental theory is limited in three areas: (1) a lack of attention paid to cultural differences in child-rearing pat-

terns of boys and girls (Symonds, 1991); (2) a lack of consideration for significant relationships that go beyond heterosexual,
genital attachment, including those between members of the same
sex or between parent and child (Kaplan, 1987); and (3) an under-
representation or exclusion of females in much of the fundamental research. As Enns (1991) pointed out in her review of models
of women's identity, prominent personality theories often were
based on empirical research with homogeneous groups of relatively privileged men. For example, Murray's (1938) theory of
psychology of needs, Perry's (1970) theory of college students'
intellectual development, Levinson's (1978) theory of adult stages
of development, and Kohlberg's (1981) theory of moral development all were based primarily on studies of males.

In light of these serious omissions, it comes as no surprise that traditional theorists from Freud on have encountered
difficulty fitting women into their prevailing theories, echoing
Freud's confession to an "unsatisfactory, incomplete, and vague
insight into developmental processes in girls" ([1924] 1973, p. 94).
Developmental theories have provided valuable insights on human
behavior, but the exclusion of women's experiences has encouraged too narrow a view of mental health. When women are as-
sessed in terms of traditional theories, they are often found to
be developmentally deficient. Thus, Freud found women to be
genitally inferior (real or imagined) and to have a poor super-
ego, and Erikson found women to have dependency problems.
Kohlberg found women to be morally unsophisticated, rarely
achieving beyond a score of three on a possible scale of six on
measures of moral development (Symonds, 1991).

Women have been protesting this masculine bias in psychology since the infancy of psychoanalysis. Karen Horney was
one of the first female challengers of the male bias in psychoanalytic thinking. In the 1920s and 1930s, she attempted to add
to or revise Freud's theory. Horney took exception to the practice
of equating what is normal for human beings with what is normal for males. Her collection of papers pertaining to feminine
psychology are "full of momentous questions and groping answers" (Eckardt, 1991). For example, the assumption that females
feel at a disadvantage because of their genital organs was so

objectionable to Horney that she speculated it was due to male narcissism that one half of the human race is assumed to be discontented with its assigned sex. Other themes broached or elaborated by Horney during this early phase of her psychoanalytic writings included that female and male biology are different but equal, that the depreciation of motherhood may result from the male's overcompensation for his relatively small role in procreation, and that the male's fear and disparagement of women have held across cultures and throughout time.

Fifty years after Horney's early contribution to feminine psychology, feminist thinkers continue to question the tradition of measuring mental health from a male orientation that emphasizes separation and autonomy but neglects the "intricacies of human interconnection" (Miller, 1988, p. 1). Within the past fifteen years, a reinterpretation of current psychoanalytic thinking that argues for new principles of the development of the self has emerged. The most central theme to come out of this work is the importance of connection and relatedness to women's lives, a dimension of development historically relegated to second-class status by the traditional theorists (Kaplan, 1987).

## Growth Through Connection

Using the early pioneering work of Jean Baker Miller (1976), the scholars at the Stone Center for Developmental Services and Studies have reformulated developmental theory in order to include women's experience. The central theme of this theory emphasizes "that the direction of growth is not toward greater degrees of autonomy or individuation and the breaking of emotional ties, but toward a process of growth within relationship, where both or all people involved are encouraged and challenged to maintain connection and to foster, adapt and change with the growth of the other" (Surrey, 1985, p. 8).

These researchers originally called their theory the *self-in-relation* model. They later dropped the reference of "self" to focus more on the relational dimensions. The core of their model is empathy and growth through connection. The relational development model posits that the development of a sense of self for women must be understood within the context of the development of relational capacities.

## Mother-Daughter Connection

Traditionally the male's separation from the female caretaker was believed to facilitate the development of an internal sense of one's self. In fact, much of the psychoanalytic literature suggests that girls cannot develop an internal sense of self because they are the same gender as the primary caretaker. According to Miller, casting mother-daughter relationships in problematic and negative terms distorts the importance of emotional connections as the basis of all continuing psychological growth. Miller says that the notion that daughters must separate from mothers is misguided because women never fully separate from their mothers, and the relationship remains crucial throughout the lives of women. Since mothers experience their daughters as similar and continuous with themselves, the relationship between mothers and daughters carries expectations of mutual empathy and interdependency. The mother-daughter relationship is the earliest model of the self-in-relation and is the foundation for empathic development, according to Janet Surrey (1985). "Through the girl's awareness and identification with her mother as the 'mothering one' and through the mother's interest in being understood and cared for, the daughter as well as the mother becomes mobilized to care for, respond to, or attend to the well-being and development of the other. Moreover, they care for and *take care of the relationship* between them" (p. 5).

Moving through the stages of life, girls use their abilities and resources to form, maintain, deepen, and enlarge their understandings of themselves and others within their relationships. Instead of developing a sense of separation, girls develop a vast and rich array of feelings, actions, responses, and influential capacities that occur within their increasingly complex relational configurations. In their play, girls' conversation is socially binding and serves a double agenda: to be accommodating and protective of the relationship, while pursuing their own ends. Maccoby (1990) reports that girls "are more likely than boys to express agreement with what another speaker has just said, pause to give another girl a chance to speak, or when starting a speaking turn, acknowledge a point previously made by another speaker" (p. 516). This style of interaction is labeled enabling or facilitative (as opposed to constricting or restrictive) and contributes to the adolescent and adult woman's capacity to form intimate and integrated relationships.

In adolescence, the relationship process between parents and daughter becomes a formative model in the daughter's evolving relational self (Kaplan and Klein, 1985). Adolescent girls do not necessarily want to separate from their parents, but instead want to redefine the relationship so that it acknowledges their developmental changes and frees them to develop new relationships that may take priority. They seek independence *within* their relationships. But for most girls, the notion of independence may be similar to confidence or self-respect; it rarely implies unattachment or disconnection (Mendelsohn, 1990). For this reason, primary concerns of separation and relationships are not experienced as incompatible by teenage girls. Rather, they may be seen as coexistent and even complementary.

If this need to continue to take care of yet change the relationship is not honored, both mother and daughter may experience shame or a diminished self-worth (Surrey, 1985). By renegotiating her relationship with her parents, the adolescent girl increases her potential for mutual empathy, relational flexibility, relational conflict resolution, and mutual empowerment (Kaplan and Klein, 1985). Therefore, her ongoing, yet changing, connection with her mother becomes a crucial factor in her self-development. Developmental difficulties may occur when the girl is unable to remain connected while she develops a differentiated self-concept.

## Renegotiating Connections

The woman's struggle to renegotiate her relationships continues into adulthood, with added complications. Women are more likely to blame themselves for relationship failures because they are so invested in building relationships. Often the woman's focus on relationships is misconstrued as dependency, regression, control, or intrusion. But the woman's wish to be in relationship is not a wish for continued dependence and avoidance of independence. Rather, it is a desire to establish intimacy with another, to comprehend the other, to understand the feelings of the other, and to contribute to the other's growth and development. Jordan (1986) refers to this desire as mutuality, "a real interest in the subjective experience of the other" (p. 11).

The words of our women psychotherapists suggest that many of them changed their relationships with their mothers and gained an independence while still benefiting from the positive maternal influence. One daughter used a maternal example of protective control to gain more independence for herself: "I was her favorite and she felt that she knew what was best for me. This was good as a child, but not as an adolescent and young adult. Her strength challenged me to not follow what she said but to carve out my own way."

We can see in their recasting of negative parenting experiences into positive lessons the women's desire to remain connected yet become more independent. Several women referred to learning how *not* to live their lives from observing their mothers' situations. For example, "[She was] an example that I fought to be different from," and "I saw she felt constricted and unhappy with the limited range of options available to her."

Values derived from their family of origin became important to these women psychotherapists and to their work. Some of these values, such as achievement, honesty, and compassion, directly carried over from their families to their work. Others (for example, financial security) may have been valued by the family but were not important to their work. And still other values (for instance, spirituality) were central to their work but had not been recognized as family values. This process of adhering to some family values while adapting others to fit their needs and identifying their own values as distinct from those of the family is indicative of how these women changed their relationships, remaining connected yet developing independence.

## An Ethic of Responsibility and Care

Kohlberg's model of moral development views the relational bias in women's thinking as an impediment to women's moral judgment. According to Kohlberg, women's care for and sensitivity to the needs of others infuse their judgments with too much emotion so that they are incapable of developing abstract principles of justice. Thus, women's compassion and care mark them as deficient in moral development, often limiting their moral reasoning to stage three of Kohlberg's six-stage scoring system. Stage three is described as being oriented to pleasing or helping others for the purpose of gaining their approval.

Through her work with Kohlberg and Erikson, Carol Gilligan became aware of the male bias in the critical theory-building studies of psychological research. Her landmark book, *In a Different Voice* (1982), drew attention to the variations in women's ways of speaking about morality and identity. In so doing, Gilligan amplified the extent to which developmental theories have drawn heavily from men's experience: "As we have listened for centuries to the voices of men and the theories of development that their experience informs, so we have come more recently to notice not only the silence of women but the difficulty in hearing what they say when they speak" (p. 173).

Through her research on women, Gilligan delineated the growth of an ethic of responsibility and care. She discovered that women's morality is connected to responsibility in relationships, and that their moral reasoning assumes a connection between self and others, unlike men who tend to look at moral issues in terms of rights of individuals to noninterference. In the female voice, "the moral person is one who helps others; goodness is service, meeting one's obligations and responsibilities to others, if possible, without sacrificing oneself" (1977, p. 486). The common thread that runs throughout women's morality "is

the wish not to hurt others, and the hope that in morality lies
a way of solving conflicts so that no one will get hurt" (p. 486).

From interviews with twenty-nine women who were considering whether to continue or abort a pregnancy and from
their resolutions to the hypothetical dilemmas used in Kohlberg's
research, Gilligan was able to describe three distinct ways in
which women talked about care. The women's responses suggested a pattern of increasingly sophisticated understanding
about the nature of relationships. Gilligan found that, developmentally, the focus of women's thinking about care shifts from
the self to the other and then from the other to the relationship.
"The development of women's moral judgment appears to proceed from an initial concern with survival, to a focus on goodness, and finally to a principled understanding of nonviolence
as the most adequate guide to the just resolution of moral conflicts" (1977, p. 515).

### Self-Survival

Women at the first level — Orientation to Individual Survival —
felt alone in the world and uncared for. For them, relationships
were disappointing. Their concerns centered pragmatically on
the self and survival. Morality was perceived as externally imposed sanctions by a society that treated them as subjects rather
than citizens. In order to protect themselves against further hurt,
these women often chose isolation. In part, their pregnancies
were attempts at connection, in the hope that their babies would
care for them.

In the transition that follows this position, the woman's
attachment or connection to others redefines her understanding of selfishness and responsibility. She believes that the judgment to focus only on self-interest is selfish. Her emerging sense
of responsibility signals a deeper connection between herself and
others and is fused by a maternal morality that seeks to care
for and protect the dependent. Although the pregnancy confirms
both feminity and adulthood at this crossroads, the abortion decision becomes an opportunity for the adult exercise of responsible choice. This transition, therefore, marks an enhancement

in self-worth because the woman is able to see herself as having the potential to do the right thing. The capacity for doing good makes her worthy of social inclusion.

## Self-Sacrifice as Caring

The transition from selfishness to responsibility also signals a move toward social participation. Women at the second level — Goodness as Self-Sacrifice — base their moral judgments on societal values and norms. Their survival depends on others' acceptance and approval. These women adopt the conventional image of femininity that defines caring for others as responsible and caring for oneself as selfish. This equation of goodness with self-sacrifice powerfully affects these women's lives. The strength of this position lies in the capacity for caring for and protecting others, yet its limitation is the constraint the woman places on direct expression. "Assertion becomes personally dangerous in its risk of criticism . . . as well as potentially immoral in its power to hurt" (Gilligan, 1977, p. 498). Furthermore, it carries with it the threat that women who attend to their own needs over the needs of others will be abandoned. The woman stuck at this level of moral reasoning paradoxically holds herself responsible for the actions of others, while considering others responsible for her choices. She willingly sacrifices her own needs for others in the hope that they will love and care for her. The central threat of abandonment is a problem of disconnection that often leads her to desperate efforts at connection.

In her struggles for connection, a crucial dilemma emerges: how to include both self and others. The second transition begins with the reconsideration of the logic of self-sacrifice in the service of a morality of care. Questions of responsibility to oneself as well as to others are raised along with the possibility of reconciling the disparity between hurt and care.

Several of our women psychotherapists appeared to be in the process of struggling with this dilemma of responsibility to self versus responsibility to others. These words directly express the conflict: "I have been personally struggling with this [issue] as I have recognized I 'control' others by 'helping them.'

I am trying to 'let go' of 'feeling overly responsible' for others. In my profession I learned to let go . . . but in my personal life this has been an extreme problem."

Instead of feminine goodness, women's moral judgments shift to honesty and truth. Approval from others becomes less important than the realities of intention and consequences. By deliberately uncovering and acknowledging their own needs, women start to include themselves among the people deserving of their care. As they separate care from self-sacrifice, women begin to accept conflict and ambiguity, since the clearly "right" solution to problems that arise in relationships is often non-existent. Once again, transition hinges on self-worth, because the woman sees herself as capable of independent judgment and entitled to her own point of view. The words of one family therapist from our sample reflect these feelings of self-worth in the act of caring: "My clients have repeatedly shown me that the slings [and] arrows of unjustly deserved life events lead to such deep wounds that the scars are often eradicable. I try to always remember to reach within a framework of rationality and justice but I do not surrender my right to react."

### Commitment to Caring

The issues of the third level — The Morality of Nonviolence — concern the worth of the self in relation to others, the claiming of the power to choose, and the acceptance of responsibility for those choices. At this level of moral reasoning, women adopt a moral equality between self and other that governs all moral judgment and action. Moral decisions are optimally based on three ingredients: first, knowledge of the self, the other, and the situation; second, anticipation of consequences; and third, a course of action that is not likely to cause suffering and hurt. This moral perspective reflects a sophisticated knowledge of relationships, as well as the interdependence of the self and others. "Responsibility for care then includes both self and other, and the obligation not to hurt, freed from conventional constraints, is reconstructed as a universal guide to moral choice" (Gilligan, 1977, p. 507).

This commitment to caring for the self as well as the other is echoed throughout the responses in the questionnaire. You will hear them among the pages to come. The women appreciate the interdependence of relationships and value what they get from their clients as much as what they give to them. Some of the women mentioned having to make a choice between being responsible to self or to others. Changing or curtailing their practice in order to prevent burnout is a decision most psycho‑ therapists are faced with at some point. It is a decision based on the morality of nonviolence—not doing harm to others— and is represented in this woman's words: "I must value myself and not give myself away. I am very happy to be supervising and not seeing patients at present, as I have some energy left over for me." Burned-out psychotherapists can do more harm than good if they continue to practice. Those who take care of themselves are more likely to be able to take care of others.

## Knowing Ways of Cognitive Development

Inspired by the theories and research of Carol Gilligan and William Perry, authors Mary Belenky, Blythe Clinchy, Nancy Goldberger, and Jill Tarule (1986) examined the ways in which women view reality and come to understand truth, knowledge, and authority. Their conclusions, drawn from extensive interviews with 135 women of varying backgrounds in the late 1970s, form the basis for the book *Women's Ways of Knowing: The Development of Self, Voice and Mind.* The authors organized their observations into five major epistemological positions: silence, received knowledge, subjective knowledge, procedural knowledge, and constructed knowledge.

In the first category, Silence, "women experience themselves as mindless and voiceless and subject to the whims of external authority" (Belenky, Clinchy, Goldberger, and Tarule, p. 15), not unlike those women at the first level of Gilligan's moral reasoning perspective. These silent women who lack confidence in themselves as knowers feel powerless and dependent on others for survival. Their passivity and perceived incompetence underscore their dependence and deference to authority.

To speak out in protest would violate their conceptions of woman-
hood. The extent to which these women have been the victims
of sexual and physical abuse is notable.

Received Knowledge is the second perspective, "from
which women conceive of themselves as capable of receiving,
even reproducing, knowledge from the all-knowing external authorities but not capable of creating knowledge on their own"
(p. 15). Often childbirth is the catalyst for these women to develop their creative potentials. Turning to experts, these new
mothers open up to all of the knowledge these authorities have
to offer. The women are active listeners, quieting their own
voices so that they can hear others voice the right answers, the
truth. The dualistic outlook that things are either right or wrong,
true or false, black or white, characterizes the received knower,
just as it defines the polaristic thinkers in the initial stages of
Perry's scheme of intellectual development. Because of this either/
or mentality, ambiguity is intolerable. Received knowers are
literal-minded students who crave predictability and clarity.
They see themselves as repositories of outside knowledge, stor-
ing it in exactly the way it is received.

In moral conflicts between self and others, received knowers conform to conventional standards of femininity. Believing
that they must always choose one or the other but not both, they
resolve self–other conflicts by choosing others. The central theme
to emerge in their moral thinking parallels Gilligan's observations of women at the second perspective of moral reasoning:
that goodness is defined by the selfless care and devotion to
others. Of particular importance to women at the received knowledge position is the strength that they derive from empowering
others. Empowerment may take the form of teaching, helping,
listening to, or understanding others. Paradoxically, it is the
act of giving, rather than receiving, that strengthens their own
capacities for learning and knowing. Being responsible for another may be necessary for the received knower to shed her passive dependency on others for "truth."

Until they can listen to their own voices with confidence
and clarity, these women must rely on others for knowledge,
direction, and care. Their steadfast belief that all knowledge

originates outside of themselves puts them at the mercy of authorities' judgments. These received knowers define themselves through the eyes of others and try to live up to the images that others hold of them.

## Finding Their Voices

As women start to abandon their voicelessness and develop a protesting inner voice, they shift into the perspective of Subjective Knowledge, "from which truth and knowledge are conceived of as personal, private and subjectively known or intuited" (Belenky, Clinchy, Goldberger, and Tarule, p. 15). With subjectivism, the voice within remains small, but it signals the existence of inner resources. This discovery reverberates throughout the woman's relationships, self-esteem, morality, and actions, because it is "accompanied by an increased experience of strength, optimism, and self-value" (p. 83).

When women make the transition into subjectivism, the value they place on personal, firsthand experience increases. Their strategies for knowing grow out of their relationships and their awareness of the details of ordinary life. By seeking the wisdom of grandmothers, mothers, and other nurturant authorities, the women feel that they too may possess valuable knowledge. "Although they have not yet realized the power of their own minds and are reluctant to generalize from their experience to advise others, they begin to feel that they can rely on their experience and 'what feels right' to them as an important asset in making decisions for themselves" (p. 61).

It is unknown why some women are not able to move beyond the reliance on feeling and intuition for some answers and on the wisdom of external authorities for others, while other women learn to abandon both absolutism and subjectivism in favor of reasoned reflection. Those women who achieve a voice of reason shift into a Procedural Knowledge position, one of investment in "learning and applying objective procedures for obtaining and communicating knowledge" (p. 15). The authors describe the striking change in voice of these procedural knowers: "Now they argue that intuitions may deceive; that gut reactions can be irresponsible and no one's gut feeling is infallible; that some truths are truer than others; that they can know things they have never seen or touched; that truth can be shared; and that expertise can be respected" (p. 93).

Eventually the acquisition of reason and objective thought empower proceduralists with a sense of control and competitive potential. Their new mode of thinking also allows them to understand the opinions of others and "achieve a kind of harmony with another person in spite of difference and distance" (p. 101). Borrowing from Gilligan, this type of epistemological orientation that seeks understanding as its goal is referred to as *connected knowledge*. By contrast, *separate knowledge* seeks proof based on impersonal procedures for establishing truth. Separate and connected knowing are not gender specific but probably are gender related. Women may be more likely than men to try to uncover the experiential logic behind others' ideas and to learn through empathy. In the words of one family therapist from our sample, "What I have learned is humility (that I only have one perspective; I don't have a corner on truth)." It may be more usual for men, on the other hand, to apply techniques of critical analysis to uncover specious reasoning in one's arguments and to find rational grounds for disagreement.

### Connecting Reason and Emotion

As they weave together objective and subjective thought, healing the split between emotion and rationality, women arrive at the core premise of Constructed Knowledge: Truth is contextual; knowledge can be created and shared. Constructivist women come to understand that knowledge is relative and that truth is embedded in context, and this discovery unleashes a passion for learning. Because constructed knowers are active participants in the construction of truth, self-awareness becomes their guidepost for finding "points of connection between what they are trying to understand and their own expertise" (Belenky, Clinchy, Goldberger, and Tarule, 1986, p. 141).

The voices of constructivist women echo the "different voices" that Gilligan heard. Gilligan listened to women who sought to resolve conflict in the context of each party's perspective, needs, and aims — and in so doing invoke the least amount of pain. In the case of constructivists, the moral response is also a caring response, and the women aspire to transform their caring into a commitment to community and relationships. Commenting on their desire to make a difference in the world, Belenky and her coauthors noted, "More than any other group of women in this study, the constructivists feel a part of the effort to address with others the burning issues of the day and to contribute as best they can" (p. 152).

Constructed knowledge is evidenced in our sample in the ways the women express their understanding of human behavior and how to be effective psychotherapists. They have learned from their life experiences, and they respect their intuition. As one woman said, "Being female I approach therapy (and almost everything else) intuitively and holistically. I am open to being touched by others, and my nurturing instincts have been rewarded." These words also reflect a mutual empathy and reciprocity in the therapy relationship.

They have learned from their training programs about how people grow and change. The therapists combine these insights, applying what seems to work in a given situation. The following words demonstrate this combination. "I think women understand intimacy and this is taught through the generation[s] of women. Women are experts here, and therefore intuition can help guide in the therapist's process. This natural [ability] combined with a theoretical base is most powerful."

Their eagerness to learn and grow is especially piqued by the work they do as psychotherapists. It stretches them and taps their creative energy. "Every day I discover things about people. Rather, we—the client and I—have insights. And I stretch my emotional array." The reciprocity of the learning is clear in these words: "I find sometimes that when I'm clarifying or suggesting for clients, that I get clear on my own situations. It helps me to claim and know what I know when I hear myself say wise things to clients."

## If Freud Were a Feminist . . .

Luise Eichenbaum and Susie Orbach, psychotherapists, cofounders of the Women's Therapy Centre (New York and London), and coauthors of *Between Women* (1987), have examined women's relationships in depth: "women's strong and loving feelings for one another and the enmity that could suddenly occur" (p. 4). They have knitted together the threads of feminism and psychoanalysis into a unique perspective on psychological development.

According to these authors, women develop their senses of self through their connection and attachment to others. They learn about themselves by living in a network of relationships. Their relationships are nurturing, supportive, and cooperative. But the undercurrent of women's positive feelings toward each other is charged with equally powerful negative emotions: pain, envy, competition, guilt, anger, and betrayal. Part of the complexities of female relationships is due to current social forces. Women juggling the demands of career and family are forced to let friendships drift away, the price paid for overscheduled lives. Concrete differences in women's lives also create barriers to friendships. Single women may crave a different kind of companionship than married women, as might women in the work force versus women working in the home.

But beyond the recent changes in women's social position, the developmental processes for both intimacy and the difficulties in women's relationships share common roots in women's psychology. Connectedness, attachment, affiliation, and selflessness remain at the heart of women's experience. At the same time, women are struggling to become more autonomous. It is this important struggle for change that makes the texture of women's relationships so complex. "The change from a social role in which the mandate was connection to others, availability to others, self-deference and support for others, to a role that includes self-actualization, self-interest, entitlement, and desire for a place in the world as well as in the family, requires differentiation. And differentiation defies the very essence of feminine psychology" (Eichenbaum and Orbach, p. 50).

From an intrapsychic viewpoint, the origins of women's relational skills are found in the mother-daughter relationship. The mother-daughter dyad represents the microcosm of the female's relationship to the world around her. In infancy, the baby exists in a merged state with the mother. Inconsistency and confusion are intrinsic to this merged attachment because the mother cannot provide a safe, protective, and soothing environment for the infant at all times. Of course, infant sons also experience the disappointment, pain, and fear as well as the safety of the merged attachment, but they do not evoke the same projections from the mother as the infant girls do. The gender difference between mother and son provides clear-cut boundaries for differentiation, but when the mother looks at her daughter, she sees herself. The daughter attempts to make sense of her mother's variable attention to her needs. Consequently, daughters identify with that aspect of mothers that is feared and resented: the fact that they are incapable of meeting all of the infant's needs. Anger originally directed at the mother gets turned inward.

### Merged Attachments

The psychological expectations conveyed to the daughter as she grows up are, first, that her selfhood must develop out of her identification with and adjustment to the needs of others, and, second, that her mother's need for attachment to her daughter is crucial to the mother's psychological selfhood. "The mother's need for attachment, combined with her identification with her daughter, creates a fusion between the two of them (a merged attachment). The mother is not separate from her daughter and as her daughter expresses her needs, the mother experiences them *with* her, almost as though they were *her own*" (Eichenbaum and Orbach, p. 62). Individual needs, or individual development, are a threat. As a result of the merged attachment, the daughter's sense of selfhood is based on compulsive attending to others, the repression of her own initiatives, and the denial of difference. The unhealthy consequence of a merged attachment is an enmeshed relationship in which the daughter assumes responsibility for serving the needs of her mother and keeping her mother happy, which is in turn encouraged by the mother. Enmeshment leaves each person feeling inadequate without the other, incomplete, and, therefore, dependent on the other for her sense of self and security. It is the daughter's deep neediness that "invokes in her a capacity to identify with, emotionally register, and respond to the neediness of others" (p. 61). Many women may direct these feelings into taking care of others, as mothers or even as mental health professionals.

Moving from merged attachments to separated attachments becomes each woman's psychological task. Only by acknowledging and expressiong "the wanting, the longing, the desire for self-actualization, the rage at restrictions and oppression" (p. 202) can women create the opportunity to feel whole within themselves and to feel secure in their attachments, to be "separate, individuated people who were also empathic, care giving, loving, and connected" (p. 200).

This struggle to be separate yet connected is evident as women in our sample responded to the question about what was helpful (or not helpful) about growing up as a female in their families. The following words reflect a very traditional female socialization: "I was taught to do something for someone every day. To help others and help make others happy. I was also taught to share whatever I have to help someone." This woman did not seem to experience the limitations of what appears to be merged attachment. She found these lessons helpful in her work: "My clients always felt that I was most understanding and always helpful." Other women worked hard to separate from the cultural expectation to be the selfless caretaker: "[Growing up female] sensitized me to the impact of being devalued, the power of devaluing oneself, and the distinctive power of denied rage. . . . This as often hinders as helps." Many of the women succeeded in becoming separate yet connected: "Being a female was initially constricting in my power as a therapist — too caretaking — not able to set firm limits — I'm much more powerful now. My gentleness as a woman always helped me be effective."

According to family therapists Marianne Walters, Betty Carter, Peggy Papp, and Olga Silverstein in their book *The Invisible Web* (1988), mothers raising daughters do so within a set of culturally imposed double binds: "A mother wants her daughter to be able to define her own needs as an adult independent self, but she will be plagued by doubts, knowing that it is not wise for her daughter to become too autonomous, and that she must learn dependent ways" (p. 42). It is inevitable that the special knowledge mothers possess about expectations of women and social appropriateness in a male-centered world influence the lessons mothers impart to their daughters. Small wonder that mothers are cautious, conflicted, and ambivalent about empowering daughters. "The conflict mothers and daughters may experience living in a male-dominant society has been turned inward, locking them in a struggle with each other, blaming each other for whatever goes wrong in their lives" (p. 47).

## Crisis and Commitment in Identity Formation

Ruthellen Josselson, in her book *Finding Herself: Pathways to Identity Development in Women* (1987), observes that the outline of a woman's identity by the end of adolescence forms the template for her future. Through extensive interviews of college seniors between 1971 and 1973, and follow-up interviews twelve years later, Josselson attempts to answer the questions of how women form identities and how they determine what they most deeply want. Using the four identity-status groups developed by Marcia (1966), Josselson examines the internal and developmental origins of identity formation in women.

According to Marcia, the four identity statuses are defined by the presence or absence of crisis and commitment in two areas: occupation and ideology. Individuals who have experienced a decision-making period and are reaching toward self-chosen occupation and ideological goals are *Identity Achievements*. *Foreclosures* are also committed to occupational and ideological positions, but these positions are chosen by parents rather than self-chosen. As a result, there is little or no evidence of a decision-making crisis period. Irrespective of whether or not they have experienced a decision-making period, *Identity Diffusions* have no set occupational or ideological direction, "no crisis, no commitment" (Josselson, p. 140). *Moratoriums* are those individuals who are in the throes of an identity crisis as they struggle with occupational and/or ideological issues.

Josselson characterizes the female Foreclosures in her studies as the "purveyors of the heritage" (p. 42). Though not particularly insightful or emotionally complex, these are the

women whose lives are guided by a strong sense of family, tradition, and moral values. Their growth is the result of their strong
identification with their parents' values and patterns rather than
through an internal push toward self-discovery or individuation.
For some, Foreclosure marks a developmental beginning of the
quest for identity, but for those women who remain in this position at the end of college, Foreclosure becomes their way of life.
Why this is so may be due to the Foreclosures' failures to establish enough trustworthy relationships outside of the family. In
adulthood, they satisfy their need for security by choosing husbands who will care for them as their parents did. "Having deeply
internalized the values of their parents, remaining attached to
the religion they were raised in, finding men who will carry on
their traditions, these women carry forward into their lives the
emotional warmth and security of their childhoods" (p. 69).

### Forging an Identity

The Identity Achievements are the "pavers of the way" (p. 70)
toward a self-made identify. Unlike the Foreclosures who more or
less share a psychological commonality with one another, the Identity Achievements forge their own identities from a diversity of
factors and circumstances. Compared to their Foreclosure sisters,
these women "are, in general, more flexible, more open to experience, more firmly rooted in an internal sense of self, and, hence,
more independent of external sources of self-esteem" (p. 72).

The struggle for independence is the central theme that
distinguishes the adolescent Identity Achievements from the
other groups, yet paradoxically their independence seems to rest
on their relationships with a man. As the distance from their
parents increases, Identity Achievements choose men to anchor
and support them, yet still allow themselves to experience their
own capacities. Early adulthood is characterized by a related
struggle, the struggle for self-confidence. By testing their potentials, these women base their self-esteem on their own capacities as well as their relationships. Relationships remain primary
in the lives of Identity Achievements, yet they define themselves
through their work and interests as well. "The need to combine

self-in-the-world and self-in-relation appears to be a deep and early aspect of Identity Achievement women" (p. 103).

The Identity Achievements in our sample also have often chosen men as supporters yet derive the greatest amount of self-esteem from the combination of professional and personal accomplishments, as we will discuss in more depth in Chapter Four. Relationships have sometimes taken precedence over career but not over self-esteem. As much as they value relationships, these women recognize the threat of unhealthy ones and are able to end such relationships for the sake of self-preservation. This situation is analogous to the moral choice discussed by Gilligan as the third level, in which responsibility to self and to others is prized. The following comment provides an example of an Identity Achievement dilemma. "I am fortunate to have a wealth of friends—both male and female—as well as supportive colleagues. My family has always been close and supportive. My marriage dissolved in part due to my [career] success; however, I chose to be successful and fulfilled rather than pull back to a position where my husband would not feel threatened."

### Conflicts and Crises

For the most part, Moratoriums are more highly introspective and self-reflective than either Identity Achievements or Foreclosures. Referred to as "daughters of crisis" (Josselson, p. 106), these Moratorium women dare to test and search for new identities. The Moratorium state is induced by the adolescent's exposure to truths other than the ones she has grown up believing. Shocked by this realization, "a Moratorium embarks on a kind of crusade, determined to discover what is 'really right,' and, until she can find something to embrace or gives up the quest, she can make no choices around which to construct an identity" (p. 135).

Unlike the Identity Achievements, Moratoriums are rarely invested in personal achievement. Instead, they singularly focus on their need for relationships to replace lost identifications. Others provide approval, respect, love, alternatives, and ideas about how to live. "Each relationship provides raw material for

the endless introspection that often marks the Moratoriums"
(p. 138). If the identity formation process is not completed by
the end of college, Moratoriums appear unable to transcend their
conflicts. Their built-in support groups disband, leaving them
to flounder with their lives and struggle with their personal
conflicts.

The Identity Diffusions all appear to have wildly fluctuat-
ing and fragmented senses of self. As a result, these women are
highly susceptible to impulses and environmental forces. Because
of their loose personality organization, consistency is not de-
manded, and experience is ineffective in producing learning or
change. Josselson refers to them as "lost and sometimes found."

Josselson concludes that although identity formation in
all women is ultimately a unique process, the woman's positive
feelings about herself strongly determine which form of identity resolution she will experience. Prior to adolescence, the child
has internal parental standards of goodness and badness. The
developmental task of adolescence is to tip the psychological
balance of power away from these childhood expectations and
identifications toward a sense of competence that is independent of the praise of others. Diffusion is an undesirable state
because of its psychological disturbance, but the other pathways
represent differences in style and values. The aspects most salient
to identity construction in women are "communion, connection,
relational embeddedness, spirituality, affiliation" (p. 191).

### "Nothing Matters More"

We asked the women psychotherapists in our sample to tell us
about their relationships. Our questions explored how their relationships with others helped or hindered them as psychotherapists, to what extent they used in other relationships the skills
they learned as psychotherapists, and what role relationships
have played in their career and life decisions. We asked them
about their experiences as psychotherapists and mothers, daughters, wives, friends, as well as students and protégés.

Their responses echoed the words of the theorists on many
levels. Without referring to the theories, their experiences

reflected relational growth, an ethic of care, and connected knowledge. Many of their relationships had qualities of "differentiated attachment," and they clearly were "pavers of the way" as Identity Achievements.

In the words of one family therapist, "Women are cast as the caregivers — the critical part of me is inclusion of self and other in the care, valuing the relational aspect of being female . . . I'm less hierarchical in my therapy than many male therapists — females don't have much power in our society and I feel strongly about not abusing power. Women often don't have a voice, and I feel strongly about discovering my own voice and helping clients do the same."

The speaker's reference to "the inclusion of self and other in the care, valuing the relational aspect of being female" speaks to mutuality and growth through connection. Concerns about one's responsibility toward others are heard in the words about not wanting to contribute to society's abuse of power over women and taking a nonhierarchical stance. The commitment to community and to making a contribution to others is heard in the desire to discover her own voice and help others do the same. Collectively, the words demonstrate a struggle for self-confidence acquired through a sense of self-in-the-world and self-in-relation.

In response to the question, "How has the centrality of relationships affected your life decisions and sense of yourself?" the majority of the women in our sample agreed: nothing mattered more. As one woman said, "The loving relationships I have had [have] increased my sense of self-worth [and have] allowed me to make difficult life decisions. They replenished the wellsprings of my emotional life so I could do the kind of work I did without 'burning out.' I firmly believe it is impossible to give love unless you have received love." For another woman, relationships are a measure of self-worth: "I do not measure or evaluate myself by money or accomplishment but by how satisfying relationships are. My sense of myself depends more on relationships than anything else. . . . The security and comfort I feel in these relationships provide a buffer from the hard 'knocks' of life." Table 2.1 provides a breakdown of how responses to this questionnaire item were rated.

## Table 2.1. Centrality of Relationships.

"Recent advances in feminist pscyhotherapy have indicated that the formation and maintenance of satisfying human relationships is central to the identity and life choices of female adults in all walks of life. How has the centrality of relationships affected your life decisions and sense of yourself?"

| How central are relationships? | Responses (%) |
|---|---|
| 1 — not central | 4 |
| 2 — of moderate importance | 24 |
| 3 — very important | 67 |
| 4 — harmful effect | 5 |
| To what areas are relationships central? | |
| to career decisions | 25 |
| to sense of personal well-being | 29 |
| to "all of life" (career, personal) | 46 |

## A Basis for Life Decisions

In addition to contributing to a sense of personal well-being, human relationships become the basis on which most central life decisions are made. Jobs get chosen or left; homes and communities get abandoned; successful careers are soft-pedaled so that individuals can accommodate their lives to the lives of their beloved friends, life partners, and offspring. As this high-achieving professional woman states about the importance of human intimacy in her life, "It is my priority in life, the primary source of satisfaction and happiness. It is my definition of 'the meaning of life.' All life decisions are made with that issue in the fore. For instance, I remain in my present job because of the relationships there and the stability it provides for my family and network of friends."

Because of the relationships in these women's lives, they are able to meet the demands of their careers: "My central relationships with husband, child, friends, and pets form a personal fan club, a personal safety net of support to be relied on as needed. From this net, I am able to walk the high wire of personal and professional risk taking."

## Relationships Are First

When confronted with a choice between career and personal relationships, career will almost always be given a lower priority. The sacrifices in their careers these women have made are often done without regrets. For example, "The centrality of my relationships has led me to ultimately choose to work in more interpersonally satisfying rather than the 'most famous' environments." "Relationships have been and are key issues in my life. Work takes second place. The reason I work is to enjoy my relationships." For at least one woman, even though her relationship failed after compromising her career, she still gives her relationships top priority: "I compromised some significant career decisions to maintain a primary (and dysfunctional) male relationship. I don't regret those choices as much as I now am just aware of the centrality of that connection for me. Relationships with women friends have fed and supported me since girlhood. My connections with my children have altered my life goals and brought much satisfaction. I lost too much self in the relationship but I also learned a lot. I hope sometime to have an intense love relationship, but one which costs me less of myself."

It is the personal fulfillment, the sense of greater self-esteem, that seems to motivate these women to continue to value their relationships even at the expense of greater fame or financial success. But, as we discussed earlier in this chapter, self-esteem will not be compromised for relationships that are perceived as unhealthy. The following comment illustrates another example of the Identity Achievement's dilemma, and of a third-level moral conflict, according to Gilligan's definition: "The support from those I care about is important — I honestly believe that if I felt thwarted or discounted by husband or friends I would confront it and if the conflict would not resolve, I'd terminate the relationship rather than live meeting the needs of others to the exclusion of mine."

They seem to derive self-esteem from positive relationships but once empowered with a healthy ego will not pursue unhealthy relationships that diminish their sense of self.

For the most part, the women are happy with the influence their relationships have on their lives. Some women, however, are uncomfortable with their dependence on others and distrust themselves in relationships. "I continue to struggle with the core issue of commitment to self versus commitment to other. . . . I tend to make decisions based on a sense that I must give to others, often disregarding my own impulses to be more focused on myself." As females in our society, we are socialized to be other-oriented. As professionals in a competitive field, we are encouraged to be self-promoters. This double-bind is one experienced by many women with careers, and it can leave them stuck between the second level of Gilligan's morality structure (self-sacrifice) and the third level (responsibility to self and to others). Such a conflict can undermine the self-esteem of those who have not reconciled the ambiguity: "[Relationships] are critically important but I have always mistrusted such propensities in myself—feeling they make me too vulnerable and dependent on others."

Betty Carter, the second woman to be profiled in this book, acknowledges the role that relationships have played in her career and personal development.

### Beyond Autonomy—Elizabeth Carter

Betty Carter acts as a model for colleagues who want to make a contribution to the theory and practice of family psychotherapy. She coauthored *The Invisible Web,* about the female role in families and the advantages of being female in practicing family therapy. Betty Carter is a female pioneer who directs her own family therapy training center. She received her degree in social work in 1971 and has been active in the field of mental health for two decades.

Betty describes her early family experiences as influential in her own learning, in her personal life, and in her theoretical contributions. Betty's mother impacted on her daughter's development through her belief in education, her perseverance, her endurance, and her sense of humor. To those colleagues who have seen Betty in action, the same qualities are evident in her work and personality. The values important in Betty's family became central to her beliefs about what makes psychotherapy work. These values include helpfulness, hard work, and reliability. Betty also believes that the therapist's empathy, diagnostic skill, sense of humor, capacity to nurture, belief in human potential, and interpersonal skills are all central in enabling clients to change. Some of Betty's contributions were made in spite of a lack of parental support. She believes that her parents would have preferred that she had concentrated on marriage and parenthood and left the attainment of a successful career to her brother. However, Betty has skillfully managed both family and career and has gone on to contribute through practice and theory to the lives of younger colleagues who also want to handle both goals.

Early criticisms of feminism included the accusation that feminists were anti-male. Recent advances in feminist psychotherapy have indicated that the formation and maintenance of satisfying human relationships with both men and women is central to the identity and life choices of female adults in all walks of life. Betty is an example of someone who has put intimate relationships first throughout her life. She reports that the centrality of relationships in her life have molded her life decisions and her sense of herself. "I would never make a decision for my career or for any reason if it would jeopardize my close relationships. All growth and all development of self takes place in relationship to important others." Although this is Betty's personal statement about herself, it has also become a central theme in the more recent theories of female development.

Betty believes that being female has been basic to her power as a therapist. "Understanding how relationships work, and the priority of relationships in life, are central learnings for females and for therapists — or at least they should be." Continuing about the psychotherapy process, Betty states a basically optimistic stance in relation to the capacity for human change. "Process is what matters. Almost anything can be worked out between two people if there is good will."

Betty Carter continues to write, to teach, and to enable families to change. She is a representative for those of us who, as female psychotherapists, recognize that our professional and personal lives are deeply affected by our commitment to excellence in theory building and to the centrality of relationships in human bonding.

## The Centrality of Relationships

Women traditionally have been misunderstood in psychology. Inspired by accounts of women's experiences, many theorists are energetically exploring women's psychology. The researchers who are at the vanguard of revising mainstream theory are attempting to expunge psychology of its male bias in order to bring an essential balance to the field. One main thread that runs through their combined writings is that women's relational strengths give them a different outlook on life from that of men. Throughout the lives of women, relational connections are crucial.

The greater connectedness of females surfaces early. Early socialization, mother-daughter attachments, childhood play, and communication patterns all provide extensive training for the development of empathy and intimacy. Traditional feminine traits such as sensitivity, compassion, nurturance, and warmth seem to be the glue that holds relationships together. Critical issues for women include being responsive to others, affecting others, giving support to others, and encouraging others' confidences. It is not coincidental that these same qualities are just as essential for the professional mastery of therapeutic skills.

The experiences of the women diplomates and family therapists are consistent with what the theories of female development tell us. Their voices unanimously endorsed the crucial role that relationships play in their lives.

# 3

## What Makes Therapy Work?

*I just don't believe there is one truth — we are involved in a process of discovering the truth.*
— Carol Anderson

Hundreds of books and articles have been written and thousands of studies conducted to attempt to determine what accounts for the effectiveness of psychotherapy. Therapist variables, such as theoretical orientation and years of experience, have been examined. Client variables, such as presenting problem and length of time in therapy, have been considered. Therapist-client variables, including gender, age, and ethnic group, have been explored. In this chapter, we will highlight the relevant research as well as present the opinions of the diplomates and family therapists in our sampling regarding what makes therapy work. As we saw in Chapter Two, their opinions suggest that part of what they experience as their effectiveness as psychotherapists is related to the lessons they learned growing up female in our society and to the importance of relationships in their lives. The Stone Center writings on mutual empathy and egalitarian models of caring, discussed in Chapter Two, provide a backdrop for what the women therapists identify as the healing qualities of the therapy relationship.

## Does Therapy Work?

As professions go, psychotherapy is relatively new. The training of psychotherapists in other than psychoanalytic processes was virtually nonexistent until after World War II. The proliferation of approaches to psychotherapeutic treatment in the past three decades has raised considerable conjecture about whether psychotherapy works and, if so, exactly how and why it works, and which approach seems to do the job most effectively.

The origin of the controversy on whether psychotherapy has beneficial effects is usually traced to a 1952 article by Hans Eysenck. Eysenck, a British psychiatrist, challenged the effectiveness of psychoanalytic psychotherapy. After studying twenty-four outcome studies of 8,053 patients in psychoanalytic therapy, he concluded that two-thirds of "neurotics" improved whether or not they received treatment. Not surprisingly, Eysenck's conclusions were quickly challenged by a number of psychotherapists. The work was criticized for inaccurate research methods and the incomparability of patient and treatment variables in the twenty-four studies he correlated to arrive at his conclusions.

In contrast to Eysenck, a number of investigators have subsequently found psychotherapy to be an effective form of treatment. The most commonly cited studies are the meta-analyses conducted by Mary Lee Smith and her colleagues. Mary Lee Smith and Gene Glass (1977) published a meta-analysis of 375 controlled experiments on ten different therapeutic approaches. Their primary conclusion was that the typical client was in better mental health after therapy than 75 percent of untreated people (control group). This finding reversed Eysenck's conclusion. In 1980, Smith, Glass, and T.I. Miller conducted another meta-analysis that reviewed 475 studies of a total of 25,000 subjects and seventy-eight different forms of therapy. This time, they concluded that the typical client was in better mental health after therapy than 80 percent of untreated people. Their second major finding was that no one therapy is consistently superior to any other therapy. Similar results, including a more recent meta-analysis on the outcome of short-term psychodynamic psychotherapy, have subsequently been reported by other researchers (Crits-Christoph, 1992; Lambert, Shapiro, and Bergin, 1986). That therapy is effective but that no one treatment is consistently considered the best are two widely accepted conclusions in the field of psychotherapy today.

### What Predicts Successful Therapeutic Outcome?

Human change, other than specific behaviors, is extremely difficult to measure in objective terms. A proliferation of approaches to psychotherapeutic treatment has further confused the question of what makes therapy work. For example, it has been estimated that there are already 250 schools of therapy, and new therapies are continually being developed. Furthermore, there is a growing trend toward eclecticism in psychotherapy, partly due to the lack of evidence consistently supporting one treatment over another, and partly in response to the growing pressure for accountability by third-party payees and other consumers. Many well-trained psychotherapists in practice recognize the strong points of each school of psychotherapy and attempt to integrate strains of diverse techniques and concepts into a personal, comprehensive, and yet pragmatic approach that avoids strong ties to one theory. In one recent report, 68 percent of therapists described themselves as eclectic, integrating primarily psychoanalytic, humanistic, and cognitive-behavioral orientations (Jensen, Bergin, and Greaves, 1990).

Client and therapist ratings are the most commonly used criterion measures in psychotherapy outcome research. The problem here is that self-reports are biased and probably unreliable. For instance, Garfield, Prager, and Bergin (1971) found that although therapists and clients indicated an 80 percent improvement rate in their study, ratings by supervisors suggested a 56 percent improvement rate, while pre- and post-comparisons on standardized, objective assessment measures indicated essentially no improvement. All relied on reports from persons with different biases.

Much of the outcome research on client factors, therapist

factors, and client-therapist factors has likewise produced contradictory results. Overall, client variables, (for example, intelligence, education, marital status, attractiveness, level of disturbance, and expectations about the nature of therapy) seem to be
adequate predictors of therapy outcome (Frank, 1974; Luborsky,
Crits-Christoph, Mintz, and Auerbach, 1980). Most researchers
agree that therapist characteristics have not been consistently
linked to improved impact on the outcome of therapy.

   With contradictory research findings and little agreement
among the experts, how can would-be consumers have confidence that an expensive and often emotionally painful experience will result in improvement in their conditions? A good
question. Yet, the practice of psychotherapy has increased ex-
ponentially in the United States in recent decades. The growth
of the mental health profession alone provides a strong indica-
tor that psychotherapy is effective with a variety of conditions
from adjustment disorders to personality disorders. The law of
supply and demand must be telling us something.

   One explanation for the effectiveness of psychotherapy
is in the therapeutic alliance. Most therapists consider the therapeutic relationship to be an essential component of successful
therapy. In his book *The Compleat Therapist* (1991), Jeffrey Kottler
said, "the reason why all therapy works is because it satisfies
a basic need for human contact and engagement" (p. 51). He
acknowledged, as does the outcome research, that particular
therapeutic orientations do not hold the keys to effective psychotherapy. Training in a given therapeutic orientation (for example, psychodynamic, cognitive, systems) may provide structure
and a reference point for the therapist in terms of conceptualizing client issues and providing therapeutic interventions. However, the qualities that define the effective therapeutic relationship supersede any particular orientation, though some of these
qualities may be more readily identified with certain orientations than with others.

   For example, Carkhuff and Berenson (1977) identified
four qualities of effective helping relationships that are associated
with humanistic approaches, in particular Carl Rogers's client-
centered therapy. These traits are empathy, respect and positive

regard, genuineness, and concreteness. The therapist who communicates with the client with high empathy, respect, genuineness, and concreteness connects solidly in a therapeutic relationship. Subsequent research on Rogerian techniques of the therapeutic relationship concluded that these qualities are necessary but not sufficient to account for client change (Mitchell, Bozarth, and Krauft, 1977). In reviewing his own earlier research, Sloane (Sloane and Staples, 1984) said that the single most important part of treatment, according to clients, is their personal interaction with their therapist.

Other researchers have looked to the therapeutic relationship to explain the effectiveness of psychotherapy. The classic study by Fiedler (1950a, 1950b, 1951) compared therapists of psychoanalytic, Rogerian, and Adlerian orientations in an attempt to define the ideal therapeutic relationship. He concluded that level of experience rather than particular orientation accounted for more positive therapy outcome. Subsequent research (for example, Bergin and Lambert, 1978) suggested that greater therapist experience is associated with lower dropout rates. Barrett-Lennard (1962) found that more experienced therapists exhibited higher levels of the relationship qualities of empathy, congruence, unconditional positive regard, and genuineness.

Let us now turn to our own experts, the diplomates and family therapists in our sample, to find out what they believed to be predictors of successful psychotherapeutic outcome.

### Curative Factors, According to Women Therapists

To explore what makes therapy work for our psychotherapists, we included ten "curative factors in the psychotherapy process" in the "Woman as Therapist" questionnaire. Identifying curative factors in psychotherapy is a central topic in psychotherapy outcome research. In order to comprise a comprehensive yet succinct listing of those variables considered to be curative, we took several steps. We reviewed the psychotherapy outcome research literature. We drew from our combined twenty years of experience in teaching and training psychotherapists. We conducted two pilot studies of the questionnaire, one using local colleagues and one using a national sample of teachers, supervisors, and clinicians in professional psychology. Earlier forms of the questionnaire used in the pilot studies asked respondents the following question: "Some of the attributes that contribute to a therapist's effectiveness have to do with personal qualities, skills, approaches to effecting change, and viewpoints on human nature. Please list what you feel are the *three most important* attributes that account for *your* effectiveness as a therapist." The final list of "curative factors" included in the "Woman as Therapist" questionnaire resulted from compiling the results of an overview of research in the field, our knowledge of the factors exhibited in people who become successful psychotherapists, and the voices of the experts who assisted us in the pilot studies. The ten factors were as follows:

1.  *Insight* — the capacity to use intuition in perceiving the inner nature of things and of oneself
2.  *Observational skills* — the ability to gather information through various sensory channels and to discriminate among the pieces of information observed
3.  *Empathy* — the ability to sense another's feelings, thoughts, experiences from that other's frame of reference and to communicate that understanding
4.  *Diagnostic skill* — the ability to identify the presence or absence of pathology by critically studying evidence of its signs or symptoms in individuals
5.  *Sense of humor* — an appreciation of the ludicrous quality of the human condition, the ability to remain good-natured in light of human suffering
6.  *Research and theoretical foundations* — the academic body of information about psychotherapy, such as outcome research and the rationale for therapeutic approaches
7.  *Cognitive acuity* — intellectual sharpness, clarity of thinking
8.  *Capacity to nurture* — the ability to foster the development of another
9.  *Belief in human potential* — a viewpoint that people are motivated to be the best that they can be and will rise to their highest level of ability, especially when they feel support from others

10. *Interpersonal skills* — the ability to actively listen, elicit responses, give and receive feedback, self-disclose to maximize understanding

In the final questionnaire, we listed these ten factors and asked our experts to indicate how important each factor is to their effectiveness as a psychotherapist. Experts could rate each factor from 1 (not at all important) through 3 (moderately important) to 5 (critical).

In order of the importance given to each, the factors were rated as follows, from most important to least important:

Table 3.1. Curative Factors in the Psychotherapy Process.

| Factor | Rating |
|---|---|
| 1. Empathy | 4.57 |
| 2. Observational skills | 4.54 |
| 3. Belief in human potential | 4.47 |
| 4. Interpersonal skills | 4.43 |
| 5. Insight | 4.17 |
| 6. Capacity to nurture | 4.02 |
| 7. Sense of humor | 4.00 |
| 8. Diagnostic skill (tie) | 3.97 |
| 9. Cognitive acuity (tie) | 3.97 |
| 10. Research and theoretical foundations | 3.50 |

All ten factors were ranked between moderately important and critical. Although knowing about research and theoretical foundations may be important to our experts, they do not view these areas as critical to their effectiveness as psychotherapists. Similarly, diagnostic skill and cognitive acuity were rated lower than the less academic qualities, though they were still valued. Sense of humor (4.00) and capacity to nurture (4.02) came in seventh and sixth respectively. Insight (4.17) closely followed in fifth place. We concluded that the cognitive-affective balance represented by the clustering of these factors is what Kottler seems to be describing: "The compleat therapist is able to think as an intuitive scientist who can reason both inductively and deductively, systematically uncovering mysteries, yet who

has developed the tacit dimension, who trusts and uses inner
forms of knowing" (1991, p. 119).

The therapists were very clear that it is necessary to know
how to relate to people skillfully in order to help them change.
The clustering of the top four functions includes interpersonal
skills (4.43) and a belief in human potential (4.47) fourth and
third respectively. The therapist's belief in the client's potential
to improve has been linked in the research to positive therapy
outcome (Frank, 1973; Fish, 1973; Pentony, 1981). Kottler says,
"The essence of effective therapy is the clinician's unwavering
belief in his or her capacity to promote healing and the ability
to inspire this faith in others" (1991, p. 57).

The ability to observe human cues and behavior (4.54)
was a close second to empathy (4.57), the highest ranked factor
in the study. The experts seem to agree with Jean Baker Miller's
belief (1986) that "mutual empathy" is responsible for psychological growth. Miller described mutual empathy as "the combination of emotional responsivity and yet difference" (p. 18),
an individual's ability to connect with what the other is experiencing yet add her own thoughts and feelings, not just reflect the
other person's. That connecting and sharing provides the mutual
experience that has the potential to change both of the people
in the relationship. Said Miller, "If you attend to me and respond
with feelings and thoughts which connect and convey recognition of what I've just expressed—but which are your authenti-
cally different feelings and thoughts—I have the chance to see
and feel and think something a little different. I'm 'stretched'
a little in my actual 'life experience', enlarged in that way. And
then if I do likewise, you are too" (p. 18).

## Is Psychotherapy an Intellectual Pursuit?

Carl Whitaker once said that many activities are therapeutic
but do not constitute psychotherapy (Whitaker, conversation
with Judith M. Coché, 1981). As we reviewed the ranking of
the importance of the factors central in psychotherapy, we were
a bit surprised by what our experts told us. Research and theoretical foundations, diagnostic skill, and cognitive acuity were

ranked lower by our erudite professionals than were the dimensions of empathy, interpersonal skill, and belief in human potential.

At first we viewed this trend with bemusement. It struck us as almost paradoxical that our experts invested decades of their lives in fine-tuning research, assessment, and psychotherapeutic techniques only to downplay the centrality of these variables in their work. But data are data. For whatever reasons, which we consider worth exploring in continued research, our experts consistently describe the psychotherapy process as a healing of past wounds and human isolation through stable contact with a valued professional psychotherapist. We are reminded of one of our clients, a female artist who has exhibited nationally, who believes that all of her years of formal training provide a foundation but that her work is created through an almost spontaneous process in which intellect becomes the maidservant to emotionality. In a similar fashion, our experts integrate their academic training in performing what they consider a healing art.

## Is Therapy a Healing Art?

The importance placed on empathy, belief in the potential for growth, and interpersonal skills is echoed in our experts' responses to the question: "As a professional therapist, what do you believe to be healing about human relationships? How do you use yourself in the therapeutic relationship to produce healing?"

In our questionnaire, we included both scientific and healing language in relation to the activity of psychotherapy. We were curious to see how women would refer to themselves and the process of their work. The relationship between the psychotherapy process and the healing process is dear to the hearts of these wise and powerful diplomates and family therapists. Because our respondents were clear that their work involves healing old wounds for clients, we will use this voice as we talk about their work. The qualities they associated with healing include empathy, honesty, love, connectedness, and mutuality.

## Empathy

One of our experts wrote, "The healing aspect of human relationships, I believe, is the *empathy bond*—that someone really
understands how you feel and that understanding is communi-
cated to the patient." A retired mother of three responded, "The
healing power of empathy and understanding. Knowing when
to be there *with* the patient, when to be there *for* the patient,
and when to stand aside."

The experts have learned that, in order to grow, clients
need what all people need—understanding and acceptance of
their thoughts and emotions, regardless of the shame or intensity that might be associated with them. Other curative factors
frequently mentioned were support, listening skills, honesty,
authenticity, and mutual respect. Our experts' voices spoke with
a resounding YES—psychotherapy is healing.

## Honesty

One diplomate focused on the power of honesty: "[Psychother-
apy is] a relationship built on genuineness, honest caring about
the person, straightforward feedback, and belief [that] the positive force toward wholeness in each person provides an environment where the most shameful behavior can be separated from
the self and examined and the life-celebrating core allowed to
grow."

A second diplomate described this process for the client
in terms of being known: "There is a sense of being 'known'
(for better and for worse), appreciated, and being important
to someone or [to a] set of someones, of having one's views be
seen as at least worthy of attention, of having a chance to give
to another—a general sense of being valued and valuable. I
listen, appreciate, and . . . keep up the search for solutions,
guide, hold forth the notion that they have promise."

A third diplomate discussed her respect for the importance of consistency: "I have learned a lot about the wonders
of being human, and the immense pain people have to grapple
with. I have also learned about the impact of small actions, [that]

a few words can have, and the importance of being consistent, even when I don't feel like it."

## Love

Many of our experts spoke of love as crucial to the therapy process.

A sixty-three-year-old diplomate: "Love is the healing factor, a kind of love that doesn't seek personal pleasure, excitement, or reward, other than the growth and recovery of my clients."

A fifty-year-old family therapist: "Love, as defined by Scott Peck — the willingness to extend oneself for the spiritual growth of self and other."

An unmarried associate professor: "Love. I don't mean this in some sappy '60s way. I mean a love for life and for the liveliness in people."

A social worker and mother of five children: "Ability to love yet demand growth with therapist behind patient, *never* in front of."

A diplomate from the East coast: "To be accepting, loving, and giving."

## Connectedness

Others believe that human growth occurs naturally within the context of healthy relationships.

An associate professor and mother of four: "Healing is intrinsic in the process of fully being with another person."

A fifty-year-old family therapist: "Bonding with another human opens up new capacities and information about the self."

A director of training: "All growth and all development take place in relationship to others."

An unmarried diplomate from the Midwest: "Healing is produced by a special bond."

A fifty-year-old professor of psychology: "The connection itself is healing."

Another professor and mother of three: "Healing comes about as a result of one person caring for another."

*Mutuality*

Echoing Jean Baker Miller's concept of mutual empathy, many of our experts see the value of mutuality and equality in therapy.

A thirty-nine-year-old administrator: "A sense we're in it together."

A family therapist and supervisor: "I use myself . . . as an equal participant in the client/therapist system."

A thirty-nine-year-old full professor: "That human beings will be with, accompany, and share their expertise and their own struggles with each other. I use myself as a model, as a 'fellow' sister traveler in the world or one who has been going through the same thing."

A sixty-one-year-old family therapist: "I reveal myself and my values, as appropriate, to clients as they struggle to identify theirs."

A fifty-year-old family therapist and professor: "[My] use of self is to be relatively collaborative with clients."

A sixty-four-year-old diplomate: "To be authentic and to disclose my values."

A seventy-one-year-old emeritus professor: "The feeling of mutualness and equality is harder to come by in therapy, but it's something I try to develop in long-term work."

In sum, understanding the concept of psychotherapy as a healing process is complex. Healing implies illness; however, psychotherapists often see themselves as promoting change and growth rather than curing pathology. Reflecting this view, one respondent wrote, "I view myself as a *facilitator of change.* Time heals. 'Tissue' heals and people heal themselves. I can't take any credit for something as fundamental as healing."

## What Psychotherapy Is Not

Being interpersonally skillful, being attuned to the client, being a caring human person—these factors are central to doing psychotherapy. Our experts were vehemently unanimous on what psychotherapy is not—it is not being selfless. Sacrificing the self of the therapist was in no way seen as valuable in the psychotherapy enterprise. When we asked how professional caring is different from the self-sacrifice that is sometimes associated with caring for others, our experts spoke as if in one voice—professional caring is very different, they said.

Many people in the world confuse assisting others with self-sacrifice, as though the only way one person can be of assistance to another is if the first person is willing to sacrifice her own self-interests in the service of helping the other to grow. This thinking is typical of Gilligan's second level of moral development—Goodness as Self-Sacrifice. The power of guilt induced in the member who is growing is a direct consequence of this way of viewing the helping process. Our experts knew that those who put themselves last, or in a one-down position, are not contributing to a healthy relationship. An eighty-one-year-old retired diplomate stated, "Self-sacrifice encourages dependency and love/hate relations. Professional caring encourages independence and mutual respect." A sixty-one-year-old family therapist said, "I feel responsible *to* clients, not *for* them. . . . I am a transitional artifact in their lives."

Wrote a seventy-two-year-old mother of seven children, "I see self-sacrifice as not counting your own needs to be equal to the needs of others, thus there is not the negotiation that is important in interpersonal relationships." This lack of balance in self-sacrificial relationships is repeated in another response, "'Self-sacrifice' is a way of thinking about what one does for others that assumes the cost of caring is higher for one person in the relationship."

A few respondents emphasized the importance of boundaries and limits in therapy. A family therapist who directs a clinic said, "Professional caring knows about *boundaries*. Care can be given to others while having some protective limits for self at the same time." A thirty-three-year-old associate professor and clinician stated, "In caring for my clients, I maintain my integrity and always try to work within a certain set of limits, albeit flexible ones." Other respondents cautioned about "overdoing" for clients and advocated limiting the amount of responsibility we assume for others.

We may choose to make sacrifices in our personal relationships without losing our sense of self. One respondent distinguished between sacrificing in personal and professional relationships. "I would sacrifice my life if under some extreme condition it would save my son's life. But in no other relationship (than parent-child) do I consider 'sacrifice' of self obligatory or even associated with caring. Caring, professional or personal, does not diminish or threaten the self. Quite the opposite, it enhances. Professional caring is guided by the restriction that its expression be therapeutic for the client. Other relationships are not so restricted; one need not be so watchful."

Some respondents considered the question of self-sacrifice versus professional care in terms of gender. One respondent commented on male/female differences: "Free choice and control-of-self instead of the drivenness of self-sacrifice. The former is more gender specific to males and the latter to females." Another respondent emphasized the importance of setting positive examples for female clients in particular: "Being exclusively self-sacrificial is giving clients a very negative message, especially our female clients for whom we are very powerful role models. Any healthy caring, whether personal or professional, involves setting limits and self-care."

The dangers of self-sacrifice were eloquently summed up by one respondent: "Self-sacrifice brings resentment and rage which eliminates caring." It is the antithesis to professional caring.

## Is Femaleness Therapeutic?

Do women learn to be effective therapists in ways that are unique to their development as women?

The Stone Center research on mutual empathy (Jordan and others, 1991), as well as the other works cited in Chapter Two, highlights qualities in the experience of growing up female in our society that parallel qualities of effective psychotherapists. Women value relationships and connecting with others through listening and sharing, acceptance and support. To get the women therapists' views of the influence of this socialization factor on their own development, we asked them about how being raised female influenced their effectiveness as therapists. Results are reported in Table 3.2.

Table 3.2. Therapeutic Power.

| "How has being a female affected your power as a therapist? How do the lessons you learned as a daughter and a sister, a wife and a mother, guide you in your work as a professional caregiver? How helpful were those lessons to you?" | |
|---|---|
| | *Responses (%)* |
| Rejects premise of question — states that gender or power have no place in therapy and make no difference | 16 |
| Empathy, listening, nurturing — states these qualities are foundation of her power as therapist | 42 |
| Life experience — states that her power derives from experience acquired through living in the world | 22 |
| Two or more of the above categories mentioned | 20 |

Many of the women believe they are more empathic because of what they describe as being in the underdog role. They are better able to identify with oppressed, defeated feelings in others because they have "been in the same boat." In the words of one of our respondents, "Empathy comes from the oppression of wife-mothers." Another woman said, "I think that the requirement that I be self-sacrificing and focused on others in my family resulted in my decision to be a professional caregiver. Not necessarily a positive lesson or outcome." These comments are reminiscent of Eichenbaum and Orbach's explanation (1987) that families impose on daughters the responsibility of responding to others' needs. This role prevents the daughter (and the wife and mother she eventually may become) from developing the "separated attachments" that are necessary for one to develop a positive sense of self.

The idea of "power as a psychotherapist" drew many comments that embraced the notion of power and a few that denied it. Part of the discrepancy may have resulted from how respondents interpreted "power," since the term was not defined in the question. Those who thought of power as control or authority may have been represented by the 16 percent who rejected the premise that therapists are powerful. If power was thought of as ability as a therapist or influence, it may well have been a more acceptable concept.

While our experts believed that they needed to unlearn

lessons of passivity and subordination, many had to learn to accept their powerfulness and to identify themselves as powerful. These same women took their caretaking skills for granted. For example, a forty-six-year-old respondent stated, "As a female of my generation, I learned to nurture, care, give to others — but I've had to struggle with the realities of my own *power*."

"Being a female was initially constricting in my power as a therapist — [I was] too caretaking, not able to set firm limits. I'm much more powerful now. My gentleness as a woman always helped me be effective." This comment is reflective of how many of the women learned to value their caretaking skills and to use them to influence others' growth.

But learning about power has its dark side too. "[Being female] sensitized me to the impact of being devalued, the power of devaluing oneself and the distinctive power of denied rage. While this does not guide me in my work, I am very sensitive to it, and this as often hinders as helps."

Some concerns were voiced about the negative lessons of being female, such as overnurturing and self-sacrificing. But these qualities in less extreme form were seen as facilitative of being effective, or powerful, therapists.

A forty-year-old diplomate and mother of two said, "It's easier to be nurturant and empathic because these are skills I was overtly and covertly taught to use in all interpersonal relationships. My warmth and softness make most clients trust me more readily."

A thirty-three-year-old unmarried family therapist responded, "Being a woman has enabled me to feel free in combining empathy and nurturance with power."

We concluded that women psychotherapists get training in psychotherapy skills through the lessons they learn as females in our society. Does this actually give women an advantage over men in the mental health profession? The role of therapist gender in successful outcome in psychotherapy is inconclusive according to the research, as we saw in Chapter Two. We have no comparison group of male psychotherapists in our research, so we do not know what lessons they might have learned from growing up male in our society that have influenced their development as psychotherapists.

When we turn to our experts, several of them said they believe women are more naturally suited than men to be therapists. The following comments reflect this position:

"The female roles . . . all foster development of the 'curative factors' I consider essential. I believe in our society the background of men is a much poorer basic training ground for awareness and sensitivity or interpersonal skills."

"I believe that women are better therapists by and large because of their awareness of feelings, the importance of relationships, concern and empathy for others."

We cannot say that women are naturally more suited to becoming therapists than men are. In fact, women psychotherapists have to overcome common obstacles to success learned during their socialization, such as self-sacrifice and feeling unempowered. Several of the respondents recognize these drawbacks:

"My lessons were to be a caregiver and adapter — not helpful."

"I had to *unlearn* a passive, reactive role as a woman."

While being raised female in our society prepares us in the skill of empathy and in the acceptance of responsibility to others, there are many obstacles to be overcome. Many of our experts learned about the positive experience of power only after overcoming the negative experience of subordination.

## What Makes Relationships Work?

We asked the women in our sample what they learned from being in "a committed love relationship with a friend or spouse" that is useful to them as therapists. They did, indeed, draw parallels between psychotherapy relationships and personal relationships in regard to levels of intimacy that can be experienced in both. One family therapist said, "The most obvious revelation was to learn that our stories (mine and my spouse's) had commonalities with those of my clients; the names of the dance were different but we were all dancing." Another family therapist said, "I give both my friends and clients a deep sense of caring and concern. I am thoughtful as I process their communications. I can be with them as they feel their pain and deal with their conflicts and struggles."

Our experts stated that many of the same behaviors and attitudes that they find helpful in personal relationships are helpful in relationships with clients. In particular, they mention two attributes. First, the importance of acutely listening to the other person. Second, the value of tolerance, not needing to change others but rather respecting their difference and separateness. They discuss concepts of respecting, negotiating, and providing loving support. All suggest that relationships require work and that choosing to be involved with the lives of others requires responsibility.

What makes therapy work is what makes relationships work: a trust in process, the give and take of a mutual effort to move through the hard times to get to the better times, a respect for the person's own uniqueness. Their words say it best:

"[I learned] that such relationships ebb and flow and that's fine, that one has to always work to preserve a balance between what one gives and what one needs for oneself. I give my spouse lots of room and respect to grow, experiment, etc. I listen to him well. I share with him honestly my thoughts and feelings."

"I've learned to stay through the process and count on the basic goodness and love. With clients I share my capacity to envision them at their best and getting what they need."

"We can sometimes be unreasonable or unresponsive, but if we hang in there and are open to each other, those periods are trying [taxing] in the greater scheme of things; . . . we need to accept each other without trying to change the other — change comes from the self. . . . I'm happier and more myself in a relationship than I was before the relationship. Conflict can be dealt with without rupturing the relationship."

Table 3.3 represents the breakdown of responses.

Well-known as a family therapist, Carol Anderson adopted a Chilean child a couple of years ago. What she learned in her relationship as a parent to a child has been helpful to her as a clinician. She describes the experience of parenting as one of experiential learning. "I know things in my bones very differently now. I have a different level of appreciation in the relentlessness of parenting. One does the best one can, and then you let it be. It's okay to make mistakes." She reports that if she

Table 3.3. Ingredients of Commitments.

---

"What have you learned about being in a committed love relationship with a friend or spouse that is useful to you as a therapist? What do you give to your friend/ spouse that is similar to what you give to your clients?"

|  | *Responses (%)* |
|---|---|
| Listening and loving — acceptance, tolerance, patience, being honest and reliable, active listening | 59 |
| Ups and downs of relationships — good relationships have good times and tough times. It is worth working out the conflict. | 11 |
| Compromise, give and take, negotiation | 7 |
| Two or more of the above are mentioned. | 23 |

---

had known this a number of years ago, she might have advised parents somewhat differently as a clinician. Carol Anderson is our third profile.

### Family Therapy as State of the Art — Carol Anderson

Carol Anderson was almost forty years old when she received her Ph.D. degree in communication skills. Her career path represents that of a theoretician, researcher, and clinician of the highest order. She is currently a professor and administrator, a teacher and writer in the field of family therapy, and a model for many colleagues. Since 1981, when Carol received her Ph.D. degree, she has written or coedited five books. The first was called *Mastering Resistance,* followed by *Families and Schizophrenia.* For her work with families and schizophrenia, Carol was honored as A Distinguished Contributor to the Field of Family Therapy from both the American Association of Marriage and Family Therapy and the American Family Therapy Association. Carol went on to coedit *Chronic Disorders in the Family* and *Women in Families.* She is currently working on a book entitled *Single Women at Mid-Life.*

Asked about gender discrimination she experienced, Carol said, "I was asked to allow males to take credit for my work because it was more important to their career — in the late sixties and early seventies." Asked how she has successfully competed in the field of family therapy, Carol said, "I actually don't see this field as very competitive." She describes using common sense, humor, and energy as tools. Perhaps Carol does not see the field as competitive because she is at the top of it.

In a telephone interview, Judith asked Carol how her view of the psychotherapy process has been influenced by the person she is. Carol said, "I've been committed to families and values since the 1960s. I have always worked in a setting where biology was seen as more important than social learning. Since I've always looked at the importance of influence of families and learning, I have always been in the minority. At any moment, I had to be ready to defend my position." Carol has worked in hospital settings for some time.

Carol sees two elements as central to the psychotherapy process. First, she believes that therapeutic skill is based on an ability to stay involved enough with a family, to be empathic, and at the same time to remain separate enough to maintain a clinical perspective. "It is necessary to maintain distance and stay close at the same time." The second element that Carol believes to be central to psychotherapy concerns the view of self of the therapist. "One needs not to take one's self or one's life too seriously. You can't get too dogmatic—in life and in psychotherapy, one must keep an open mind. It is valuable to challenge your assumptions." Gurus, common to family psychotherapy, present a problem for the field in Carol's opinion. "I just don't believe there is one truth—we are involved in a process of discovering the truth. Our gurus sometimes get to believe that there is a truth and that they found it. This is a mistake."

How does one cope with the sizable problems that families bring into psychotherapy? Carol says, "I used to get incredibly overwhelmed with all the problems I saw. A long time ago, a mentor told me something really valuable. He said, 'You know Carol, there are really only two issues in life—there's lost and there's found—there are issues of grieving and abandonment and rejection and there are issues of partnering, intimacy, and working together.'" She continues, "A second mentor told me, when I would get overwhelmed by how much there was to attend to, 'Inch by inch, the world's a cinch. Yard by yard, it's very hard. Focus on the inches.'" Both pieces of wisdom have stayed with Carol over the years.

Judith asked Carol what she might suggest to colleagues just entering the field. She had two suggestions. First, "I am very concerned with how much women use themselves in trying to please other people. As psychotherapists, this means that women can get into a position of working nonstop. They don't get away to take time to be with themselves. This is necessary to get a perspective on how one thinks." She believes that psychotherapists need an overall theoretical map, which should be gained during their early years of academic training. After this initial map is developed, Carol suggests that psychotherapists spend a couple of years developing solid techniques so that "in a crisis you don't get caught up in emotions." She believes that the techniques will become second nature in a period of time, and that, once this happens, a therapist no longer feels in a crisis and develops wisdom. "Later, you have the wisdom because you *have* it and have *developed* it. But earlier you need the map and the techniques." Carol believes that experience provides the necessary security.

## What Therapists Learn from Their Clients

The nature of the therapy relationship implies that it is an experience that matters both to the client and to the psychotherapist. Existential psychotherapy emphasizes the role of the therapist-client relationship in determining the value of psychotherapy for both. Change is not unidirectional. Intense therapist engagement is essential to the process, and therapists can also expect to change.

The Stone Center model emphasizes the mutuality of the therapeutic relationship. "In therapy there are two active members who are both open to change through their participation in this interaction. The relationship that exists is central to the process, whether we talk about transference, 'corrective emotional experience', or empathic attunement" (Jordan and others,

1991, p. 288). Sidney Jourard says, "those who wish to leave their being and their growth unchanged should not become therapists" (Jourard, 1971, p. 150). The therapist's authenticity, her willingness to engage with the client as two people sharing a journey toward personal change, is also of issue. As Kottler says, effective therapists are skillful in "allowing the force and power of their personalities to guide what they do" (1991, p. 76).

The question we asked of the women diplomates and family therapists was, "What have you learned from your relationships with your clients that you can use to enhance other important relationships in your life?" Responses fell into three broad categories as presented in Table 3.4. Nowhere is the evidence of mutuality and connectedness more apparent than in their responses to this question. One respondent called it "reciprocal learning."

While we, as therapists, guide others through difficult decisions or life crises, we learn valuable lessons about the human struggle to survive. Sometimes we see examples of how to deal with (or how not to deal with) dilemmas we have yet to face in our future. As we guide clients through crises of divorce, retirement, aging parents, empty nests, debilitating disease, we prepare to face our own crises. "My clients teach me a great deal about the intricacies of various life experiences; they guide me [through] new phases of the life cycle, teach me the limits of theoretical models."

**Table 3.4. Reciprocal Learning.**

"What have you learned from your relationships with your clients that you can use to enhance other important relationships in your life?"

| | Responses (%) |
|---|---|
| Intellectual/cognitive — how people solve problems, about transference, rules to live by, what makes people tick | 52 |
| Breadth of being human — respect for human spirit, potential; human experience has many aspects | 33 |
| Communication — importance of good communication skills in having successful relationships | 15 |

The women grow, and become better psychotherapists, through empathizing with their clients' struggles; they learn to "practice" in their own lives what they "preach" to their clients. They are often humbled by the courage of their clients and by their realization of how minor a role the therapist plays in the drama of human change. Their comments imply that what "works" in therapy is not what the therapist does, or even who the therapist is as a caring person. Instead, the therapy hour becomes the stage on which the human struggle to thrive and survive gets enacted. The following quotes reveal some of the reciprocal learning that occurs for the psychotherapist.

From a diplomate who teaches and has a private practice: "I have learned to deepen relationships, to ask meaningful questions, not to fear really knowing someone. (I do less well in being known.) Clients have also helped me expand my understanding of what it is to be human, to see greater depths of suffering and courage than I would have seen in only my own life, to value, trust, and respect human striving."

A diplomate from California said, "People make their own decisions no matter how omniscient or otherwise omni- I may delude myself into thinking I am. . . . The hardest thing to do in 'helping' someone is often to refrain from 'helping.'"

Another expert stated, "They have extended my experience of life situations positively and negatively — like a good novel. I am grateful to my clients for extending my experience of life so I may be wiser in choices — personally and professionally."

An author and director of a clinical practice said, "I am no better or worse than the people who ask for my help. The goal of therapy and the goal of being a therapist are the same: to be more of a person."

Finally, the question of "what makes therapy work?" has been widely debated and meticulously analyzed in the past several decades. One solid finding of the research is that the quality of the relationship between the therapist and the client appears to be a central factor in effective outcome of psychotherapy.

The women diplomates and family therapists place highest value on the relationship qualities they use in their clinical work. According to them, empathy, authenticity, and a respect for the human condition are critical ingredients for effective psy-chotherapy. The majority of the women in the study believe they have an advantage in developing the skills of psychother-apy because they were socialized as females who are encouraged to be caring and intuitive. They learn about what makes ther-apy work from their relationships with others as well as from their clients. In the next chapter, we will look at the difficulties women psychotherapists experience in juggling the roles in their personal and professional lives and how they meet the challenges to be effective wives, mothers, friends, and therapists.

# 4

## The Delicate Balance
## Between Love and Work

*We didn't have any children together, but we had three
books together.*

—Emily Visher

The "person" of the therapist is a critical tool in the therapy
process, as we discussed in the previous chapter. In this chapter,
we take a closer look at the personal life of the psychotherapist
and the depth of influence personal experiences have in forming
the professional identities of the women psychotherapists in our
sample.

As women with careers, we have to juggle multiple roles.
We choose between taking a family vacation, attending a week-
long seminar that may enhance our chances for a promotion,
or combining the two. We choose between staying home to attend to a sick child or dropping him off at the sitter's so we can
keep an important appointment. For psychotherapists, who especially value the role of caretaking, this bind can be even more
difficult because we rely on similar skills and identities in both
our commitments to our families and to our clients. The lines
between the roles become blurred; our choice between a dependent child and a dependent client can become a painful conflict.

As husbands and fathers, men rarely have to contend with
the same degree of conflict because wives and mothers typically
carry the major part of the caretaker role. Men's careers are

much less affected by the interruptions and conflicts of pregnancy, child rearing, and, eventually, caring for aging parents.
"For women, however, every stage of adulthood contains conflicts
and compromises as they balance their roles at home and those
at work. Decisions such as whether and when to work full-time,
and how to find good child care must be faced and refaced. At
each point these decisions must balance with career options and
family situations" (Jeruchim and Shapiro, 1992, p. 3).

The women therapists in our sample fill many roles. They
are daughters, sisters, wives, and mothers in any number of
combinations. They are single parents and widows and divorcées
and significant others in committed relationships. Eighty percent of the respondents are or were married; 70 percent are
mothers. Given the average ages of their children and the year
these women earned their advanced degrees, most started their
families early in their professional careers, soon after their graduate programs were completed. (The average age of the oldest
child is twenty-seven; the average final degree was completed
in the 1960s.) They were in their early to mid-thirties, on the
average, when they began to have children. Many of them are
committed to both family and career. They appear to fit the
image that has been labeled "superwoman," the woman who has
it all.

Family therapist Monica McGoldrick (1987) said, "I realize now that there is no way for a woman to have it all. A certain degree of guilt and self-dissatisfaction are probably unavoid-
able for a woman committed to both career and family" (p. 39).
This may be a disturbing thought to the hundreds of thousands
of women in this country who have been socialized to believe
that the only way to feel fulfilled is to be committed to both career
and family. Do career women who are single or those who
are married and childless feel less fulfilled because they do not
qualify for superwoman status? Positive role models of a variety of life-style options are necessary for women to achieve
self-esteem. Statistics indicate that more women than ever before are choosing to remain single and/or childless or to remain
single but have children. These women's stories need to be told.

## Compositions and Improvisations

Mary Catherine Bateson is an author and teacher. In her book *Composing a Life* (1989), she wrote about the lives of four of her women friends and herself. She explored the choices these women — a psychiatrist, an engineer, a college president, an artist, and herself, an anthropologist — made regarding careers, marriage, and family. Early in the book, she said, "I found myself looking again at the patchwork of achievements both personal and professional and questioning how they fit together: whether they composed — or began to compose — a life; whether indeed the model of improvisation might prove more creative and appropriate to the twentieth century than the model of single-track ambition" (pp. 14–15). Her chapters describe lives of "ambiguity and multiplicity," of "fluidity and discontinuity."

In composing their lives, women rely on being adaptable and addressing "multiple commitments in flexible contexts" (p. 186). Women fill various roles and, thus, reach an integration of parts of themselves that are synergistic and adaptive to contemporary society. "Women's lives offer valuable models because of the very pressures that make them seem more difficult. Women have not been permitted to focus on single goals but have tended to live with ambiguity and multiplicity. It is not easy. But the rejection of ambiguity may be a rejection of the complexity of the real world in favor of some dangerously simple competitive model" (p. 184). Rather than learning to compete, women have become skilled at compromise and collaboration. Bateson says that, "having grown up expecting to be homemakers and caretakers, they still retain an understanding of interdependence" (p. 117). This understanding is carried by many women beyond their own families into their work and play in our society. "Each of these women has cared for children and shared intimacy with lovers, but instead of investing their whole lives in those relationships, they have learned modes of effectiveness that make them caretakers and homemakers beyond their own families, creating environments for growth or learning, healing or moving toward creative fulfillment, seeking authority as a means rather than as an end" (pp. 234–235).

Judith Coché thinks of her own experience as a daughter through the metaphor of composition and variation. In 1990, she presented a contribution to a seminar at the American Group Psychotherapy Association in which she addressed what she learned as a daughter with a highly creative mother:

> I come from a family of business people, academicians, professionals, and musicians. Somehow, miraculously, many members of my "clan" relate to our practice in clinical psychology and to our academic teaching and writing. However, comparing my own internal experience of my career to those of my clan members, perhaps my mother's experience is, in a strange but important way, most similar to my own sense of my clinical work. My mother made music for eight hours on most days of her adult life. She played the piano exquisitely, but rarely in public. She taught piano to those who admired her quiet skill and competence. But my mother's greatest musical passion was composing. My mother composed twelve-tonal music, and prided herself on being at the cutting edge of where she believed classical modern music to be headed. I grew up, subjected passively to lullabies by Liszt and Chopin at night — and being lulled by cacophonous twelve-tone chords as I returned each day from school. As I was growing up in this world of musical differences, it did not yet occur to me that I was, in fact, being supervised in the creative process. Day after day, year after year I watched my mother's involvement in the creating of models of musical expression intensify and deepen.

> At present, I "compose" in group psychotherapy. I create models in group psychotherapy in our studio, called Coché and Coche, and I train supervisees in the theory, research, and clinical applica-

tion of these models. Moving down the generations, my daughter, now eleven, is growing up hearing words like "split ambivalence" and "the principle of isomorphism" long before her preteen peers. And thus, the mentoring process continues from generation to generation, creeping powerfully into the person of the hungry, unsuspecting learner, until, one day, competence emerges.

We believe this metaphor of composing and improvising also describes the diplomates and family therapists in our sample. The life and career of Emily Visher, our fourth expert to be highlighted, provides another example.

## Improving Life the Second Time Around — Emily Visher

Emily Visher was born in 1918 and received her Ph.D. degree in 1958 at the age of forty. She has recently specialized in working with stepfamilies, in part, because she has learned what is involved by being part of a stepfamily. When Emily met John Visher, both she and he had four children. She says, "When we got married thirty-five years ago, we each had four children ranging in age from five to fifteen. We learned a lot . . . and we had a lot to learn." John and Emily went on to apply their own personal learnings as a married couple and as stepparents in a blended family. About their expertise in developing clinical techniques in working with stepfamilies, Emily says, "We did our field work first, then we went on to write about it."

Asked what she would say to a younger colleague about to become a stepparent, Emily had two suggestions. The first is to talk with people who are or were part of stepfamilies and do some reading on the topic. This is a way to get some idea of what has worked for other people and "to get a road map." Her second suggestion was to give lots of time to making the transition into a settled sense of being a family. "Give yourselves time to settle down. It takes a long time. Good relationships come from positive shared memories, and it takes time to create these."

Emily and John Visher have contributed three books on stepfamilies to the professional and general reading populations. Their first book, *Stepfamilies: Myths and Realities,* was followed ten years later by the recent *Old Loyalties, New Ties: Therapeutic Strategies with Stepfamilies.* Their third book is a guide for the public entitled *How to Win as a Stepfamily.* Asked what it was like to coauthor books with her husband, Emily said, "Great. We didn't have any children together but we had three books together." She explained that she and John have different working styles when they write and that working together involves adjusting to one another's professional differences. John composes on the computer, while Emily prefers paper and pencil. Their first book went rather slowly for this reason, but, "The second book went faster because John gave me an electric pencil sharpener." Emily went on to say that their working relationship is easier because they do not feel competitive with each other. The respect and admiration with which she spoke about John Visher was evident in her interview.

Emily's parents taught her to be independent and to cope with what life brought. Her family was very supportive and gave her the message, "If you want something, go for it." Her parents would have been equally proud if she had been a married woman with children or if she had been a professional person. However, there was a down side to so much independence. When she got her Ph.D. degree, "I became one more statistic, a woman who gets a divorce when she gets her Ph.D. — I had changed so much psychologically that my husband and I no longer fitted together and things didn't work well anymore." She learned much from her own psychotherapy: "I learned that perhaps my parents taught me to be too independent. Being close to someone requires interdependence. I also learned that it is okay to feel unhappy and depressed at times. Most important, I learned much about accepting my own humanity and the humanness of others."

As a mother and stepmother, she thinks of private practice as a unique way to balance love and work. The major advantage in independent practice is that "You have control over your own schedule. You can plan much better." She concluded, however, that it is necessary to choose the right husband if one wants to enjoy the delicate balance between love and work.

Emily Visher is a role model for those women who have been part of more than one marriage, found that life is indeed better once human bonding works successfully, and that the effort is worthwhile the second time around.

### Psychotherapists as Mothers

Seventy percent of our respondents have children (including a few who reported having stepchildren). The average number of children is two, while the mean age of the youngest and oldest child is twenty-two and twenty-seven respectively. The majority of those women who have children reported minimal conflict between their decisions to parent and to pursue their careers. More than twice as many women said they adjusted their careers to accommodate having children rather than waiting to begin their careers after their children were born. Only twenty-three of the entire group said they chose not to have children, in part, because of their careers. Seven women either are planning to have children (or more children) in the future or are uncertain as to whether or not to have children. Table 4.1. presents these data by percentages.

We asked, "How central in life planning was the expectation and experience of mothering in the *timing* of graduate school

**Table 4.1. Role of Marriage and Family.**

|                                                   | *Responses (%)* |
| ------------------------------------------------- | --------------- |
| Married                                           | 56.5            |
| Single                                            | 20.0            |
| Divorced                                          | 14.5            |
| Widowed                                           | 9.0             |
| Have children                                     | 70.0            |
| Adjusted career to accommodate having children    | 53.0            |
| Began career after children were born             | 29.0            |
| Chose not to have children                        | 14.0            |
| Plan to have children in future                   | 3.0             |
| Not sure whether to have children                 | 1.0             |

entrance, completion of degree, and professional involvement?"
Responses could range from 1 = "not at all" to 5 = "very central."
The actual mean response was 2.57 with 3 being labeled "some-
what" important.

For most women, parenting or the possibility of it did not
appear to have significantly deterred them from their career
paths. Furthermore, those psychotherapists who are parents
found the experience useful to them professionally in two ways.
First, *the personal knowledge* helps them better understand clients
who are struggling with challenges of parenting and helps them
develop patience with and acceptance of their own and others'
limits. Second, parenting is a *real life laboratory* that provides
opportunities for experiencing and understanding theories of
human development. Although a good deal of training focuses
on identifying and treating abnormal behaviors and personalities, our experts learned as mothers to recognize and understand, and even to expand their definition of, what is normal.
They also gained a deeper appreciation for individual differences and a more realistic picture of human possibilities.

Many of our experts draw parallels between their experience as a psychotherapist and their experience as a parent.
In fact, many women found parenting helpful to their effectiveness as a psychotherapist because of the common qualities and
skills required in both roles. As one diplomate said, "A good
therapist is like a good mom: a good listener, empathic, honest,
able to set limitations with a genuine appreciation for the person's specialness." Or, in a family therapist's voice, "Parenting
was a humbling experience, forcing me to grow, change, and
learn to accept diversity in human relationships. [I give] empathy and a listening ear as I try to hear what they are saying."
Another family therapist said, "Children have brought me in
touch with my 'softer' feminine side. I'm more patient about
change in my clients since [having had] children (mostly because of increased sense of my own limits)."

One woman lists a number of ways in which her experience as a parent made her a better psychotherapist: "Further
development of empathy, acceptance of dependence, further understanding of interdependence (more fundamentally than in

marriage), willingness to give opinions and guidance when a client is out of control, more perspective in differentiating 'problems' from 'crises', willingness to delegate responsibility when appropriate." It works both ways as well, in that the experience of being a psychotherapist helps one in the parenting role: "My education, training, and mostly my own efforts to look at family patterns has assisted in helping me to back off and respect [my son's] abilities."

Fewer than 6 percent of respondents with children found no similarity between the parent/child and therapist/client relationships. Mothers frequently mentioned the caregiving skills required in both the parent and therapist roles. A few mothers mentioned a similarity between the two ventures in encouraging autonomy and independence. A single parent said, "I give my child and clients 'unconditional positive regard.' Also [I] set limits, recognize their individuality [and] rights to control their own decisions. Parenting gives me humility, vulnerability— both are useful in understanding clients and others." One family therapist responded, "Caring, structure, empathy, patience, tolerance for independence and making their own mistakes— oh, it is so similar." Another family therapist said, "I give my clients and children a sense of appropriate boundaries, reinforcement of independent stances, and a holding environment until they are ready to branch out."

The women who are filling the dual role of mother and mental health professional report that good therapy skills and parenting skills are indeed similar. They emphasize the importance of nurturing, being trustworthy, and setting limits in both roles. They believe that what they learned in one role gave them an advantage in carrying out the other. Table 4.2 presents the percentages of responses in each category for the question from which these quotations were derived.

## Psychotherapists as Daughters

Mothers provided positive role modeling for the majority of the women therapists. The respondents mentioned their mothers' personal qualities of strength, courage, independence, and optimism

### Table 4.2. Value of Parenting Experience.

---

"If you have children, what is there in your experience of parenting that is useful to you as a therapist? What do you give to your children that is similar to what you give to your clients?"

|  | *Responses (%)* |
|---|---|
| First part of scoring was based on how parenting was useful: | |
| Personal knowledge of parenting issues | 71 |
| "Real life laboratory"—experience augments theory | 9 |
| Combination of both | 20 |
| | |
| Second part of scoring was based on identifying what skills are used in parenting and in doing psychotherapy: | |
| Caregiving skills: for example, active listening | 73 |
| Encouraging independence | 7 |
| Both of above skills mentioned in response | 14 |
| Skills required in each role are *not* similar | 6 |

---

as having the greatest impact on their development. They said their mothers demonstrated such good parenting skills as nurturance and support.

Many of the respondents also experienced the negative impacts of these relationships but learned from them nonetheless. Some examples of the effects of those "mixed reviews" can be found in the following comments.

A family therapist and mother of one child said, "My mother impacted my life in both positive and negative ways. The strongest positive impact was her work ethic and desire to improve her 'lot,' and her independent-mindedness. The negative impact relates to her verbal abuse and lack of respect and support for me as an individual with feelings and thoughts of my own."

A sixty-eight-year-old unmarried diplomate said, "She was nurturing and supportive. [She] encouraged me to go to graduate school and to be independent, as she was not. I remembered because I saw this intelligent, sensitive woman being a body slave to a less intelligent, aggressive man."

These comments also reveal women who changed their relationships with their mothers, becoming more independent but still connected.

Some mothers have provided examples of what not to be — self-denying, inhibited, critical, passive. A divorcée with no children responded, "Her youth and immaturity resulted in such poor parenting that I have spent a lifetime trying to reparent myself and other people." A widowed mother of two said, "She was critical and competitive in the female role, as she saw it, never in the area of professional achievement. I ended up feeling much more adequate as a psychologist than as a wife."

As daughters who took on hefty commitment to their own education, our experts were especially appreciative of mothers who valued education: Some mothers "insist[ed] on education . . . believe[d] that girls could do anything as well as boys." One woman talked about her mother who, at age seventy-five, received a lifetime teaching credential to teach creative writing. "She was definitely a role model who indicated that you can keep growing and changing what you do."

The respondents learned both how they wanted to be and how they did not want to be from the examples their mothers set and the quality of caretaking they provided. Table 4.3 shows the scoring of responses regarding how the mothers influenced the development of these psychotherapists.

Most of these daughters had mothers and fathers who valued both marriage and career for their children — their sons as well as their daughters. When parents did have a preference,

Table 4.3. Impact of Relationship with Mother.

"As a daughter, what do you believe to be your mother's greatest impact on your development?"

| | Responses (%) |
|---|---|
| Mixed model — conflict stated about positive and negative impact; for example, worked to be different from mother | 26.5 |
| Provided positive female role model | 22.5 |
| Modeled good parenting skills | 22.0 |
| Encouraged academic achievement, intellectual development | 4.0 |
| Two or more of above responses included | 25.0 |

both were reported to prefer marriage over career for daughters and to expect more achievement from sons than daughters. Respondents reported having to overcome family prejudice in relation to gender, career aspiration, and particularly the choice of the field of psychology. Their pain and disappointment comes through in the following comments.

A middle-aged unmarried diplomate remarked, "My mother would say, 'No one will marry you, but if you marry, you will get divorced.' My father would say, 'Learn typing. You'll always have a job.' . . . My father took his nephew and mentored him in my father's profession, as a dentist, while I sat at my father's desk taking telephone messages."

Married for thirty years and in private practice, one expert said, "[My family is] prouder regarding family and [my] *husband's* professional successes. Definitely—had I been a male— it would have been different."

A divorced professor of psychology stated, "If I were male, it would be easier for them to understand and to explain to others—'my son, the doctor.'"

From a diplomate in private practice and mother of two: "I think my parents would have liked it more had I married a doctor, rather than becoming one—but they both seem fairly proud of my accomplishments, although they don't fully understand what I do."

A wife and mother, administrator, and family therapist said, "I was given two messages: go out there and do everything right and never stop trying to do better than your best but don't leave home and don't achieve anything."

Such conflicting messages, especially in the absence of successful female role models, set women up for a fear-of-success pattern, feeling guilty if they avoid the challenge and guiltier if they excel in it. Some women cope with the ambiguity by choosing both career and marriage and identifying more closely with the less threatening role. From one who began her career after her children were born: "My own view is that I am prouder to be a good parent and have a good marriage and family life."

From these comments, it is not hard to see how these women define themselves in terms of their relationships to others.

As in the theory of female development stated in Chapter Two, self-esteem for women depends on their satisfaction with themselves in relation to their families, friends, and work associates. The breakdown of responses appears in Table 4.4.

## Fathers and Their Daughters

As intensely central to our experts' development as was the influence of their mothers, with equal importance but with somewhat less intensity, our experts spoke of the influence of their fathers on their personal and professional lives.

At one extreme, fathers represented a haven of positive identification in families in which the mothers were passive and inadequate as models. One of our experts who now teaches at the medical school of a major university credits her close relationship with her father as the foundation for her later development. "His unshakable sense of humor, his capacity to nurture beloved family members despite early poverty, his hunger for continued intellectual growth well into his eighties—these are the qualities that I learned through osmosis. Had I been dependent only on my mother, I hate to think where my daughter or I would have landed."

The downside of paternal infIluence included blatant sexism and frequent mention that the brothers' career aspirations

Table 4.4. Parental Expectations.

"In your opinion, would your family be prouder of you if you married and parented successfully or if you achieved recognition as a psychologist? Might this reaction have been different if you had been male? How?"

| | Responses (%) |
|---|---|
| No difference in parental expectations for male or female children | 45 |
| Parents expected higher achievement for male children | 36 |
| Difference in expectations but not qualified as achievement related | 13 |
| Damaging influence—respondent had to overcome family prejudice | 6 |

were taken more seriously than those of our experts. "Dad put a younger apprentice of his through medical school, but would never have considered me appropriate for the field of medicine."

Although the questionnaire requested greater detail about the mother-daughter relationship, our experts gave us an impression of what they valued from the father-daughter relationship. They described the importance of support for their growing intellect as young women, pleasure in the nurturance they received for themselves, and the value of modeling themselves after a competent and successful parent. "It's been my experience (for myself and for others I've talked to about this) that the attitude of our fathers has been extremely important in making women feel competent and strong. While many of us have received 'good mothering,' being treated as equal humans by Dad (as if we're as good as boys?!) seems to have given certain of us an important extra measure of self-confidence."

### Family Values in Therapy

Respondents were asked to list three values that were transmitted to them by their families of origin and to indicate which of these values were central to their work as psychotherapists. The family value listed most frequently was achievement or goal attainment; about 50 percent of the respondents carried that value into their work as psychotherapists. One-third of the women mentioned "caring and compassion for others" as being valued in the family, and nearly all of those said they carried this value over to their work. "Honesty" and "integrity" were values listed with similar frequency and were also influential in the psychotherapists' work. Fifteen to 20 percent mentioned "financial security" as valued, but very few said this value had influenced their work. Other values they listed as central to therapy but which were not necessarily family values included "working hard," "contributing to society," "spirituality," "respect for others," and the "importance of family."

### Multiple Roles and Self-Fulfillment

Ilana Lev-El (1983) interviewed seventeen women psychologists about their identities, roles, and aspirations. Her study suggested that the greatest sense of self-esteem for these women came from *combining* the roles of mother-wife and professional therapist. Lev-El talked about the problem of "role-overload," in which a conflict between two roles may result in the woman not feeling fulfilled by either role. On the other hand, having to choose between roles would have meant failure to achieve a sense of fulfillment, according to the women she interviewed.

The formation of a professional identity in women psychologists involved "internal changes" that constituted "an adult development phase" (Lev-El, p. 5). All of the women psychologists in her study said they would not be content to be "just wives and mothers." The changes in self-perception that were associated with their professional accomplishments included "feeling more assertive, feeling more confident, feeling less anxious and more independent, having better self-understanding and improved interpersonal relationships" (p. 10). The comments of a woman in our sample seem to reflect this developmental shift. As one woman said, "A profound career decision was based upon the fact that my husband was *not* successful in his work. I had been raised to believe that my self-esteem was tied to his success and realized that I needed to base aspects of my self-esteem on my own professional success. So I returned to school just following the birth of my third child and studied full-time and worked half-time. My sense of self-worth has been greatly enhanced by academic achievement and professional advancement."

Two primary factors contributed to Lev-El's subjects' ability to integrate nontraditional values with their parents' traditional ones: having parents who valued education and expected their children to do well in school, and relationships with mothers that were described as "difficult, painful, conflictual and ambivalent" (p. 12). Such women may have been less motivated to identify with their mothers and may have developed a perception of traditional female roles as inferior. These changes are nonetheless painful; as Lev-El says, "the woman may feel that she has lost a part of herself. She has given up the part of herself that represents her mother" (p. 6).

Most of the women in her study were also mothers themselves. They had been encouraged to add the nontraditional role of professional mental health worker to their traditional one of wife and mother. According to other research cited by Lev-El, that dual encouragement most often comes from parents who value their child's academic achievement, as well as from peer support groups, female role models, and male mentors (p. 7).

The double bind is clear: the need to be successful in multiple roles in order to feel fulfilled conflicts with the physical and emotional drain of trying to be superwoman. Coleman and Kaplan (1987) explored these conflicts between career and family as experienced by family therapists. They said, "As women who are family therapists we often feel mired in a multiple bind, balancing the influences and needs of our own families, our treatment families, our feminist beliefs, our professional identification and our feminine instincts" (p. 63). The authors point out a dilemma particular to psychotherapists rather than to other women with professional careers. Therapists use their socialization as females in their work with clients. Leaving the office after providing professional caregiving, they go home and provide child care, prepare meals, and listen to their family members, which can "constitute an at-home continuation of therapeutic behaviors rather than a change of pace" (p. 62). It is easier for roles to become intermingled and tasks to become monotonous when demands on these women remain fairly consistent both at home and work. In the words of Coleman and Kaplan, "At times it seems everyone wants 'a little piece of me' and that if it were possible to give everyone what she/he wants there would be nothing left. This is a particular problem for women who are taught to be responsive to the needs of those we love and put them ahead of ourselves. Violating this dictum may invoke intense guilt and personal questioning" (p. 73).

The mental health professions provide women with an opportunity to express the nurturing, caretaker role even if they are single or childless. Comments from the women psychotherapists in our sample attest to the intimacy of the therapy relationship and the mutuality of giving to and receiving from their clients, which is similar to what they experience in their close relationships with family members and friends. This opportunity to develop and explore relationships and to assist in enhancing the relationships in their clients' lives is one of the most rewarding aspects of being a therapist. One woman respondent said, "If I accept a person where she/he is, she/he will grow without my pushing and prodding. Once I move into a committed personal relationship, the urge to merge is sometimes overwhelming. I have watched my clients in this struggle, helped them move from deselfing, and in that process am more capable of those same moves in my own life."

Even within the role of private practitioner, a woman is balancing two models — the helping, giving, caring one of the therapist and the aggressive, competitive, ambitious one of the businesswoman. We have seen many practical reasons for women therapists to choose private practice — flexibility of schedule, higher income, avoidance of sexist practices in institutions. Yet many women therapists avoid private practice because they have not been socialized to see themselves as entrepreneurs (Bernay, 1988). Fortunately, younger women have a more diverse model of femininity or at least a greater variety of models, which permit ambition and competitiveness. Their task remains to integrate these models of aggression and nurturance. Toni Bernay says, "Both the tiger strength of nurturance and the empowering excitement of aggression and achievement are necessary for the integration and success of the complete woman practitioner" (p. 5). To see nurturance as "strength" and aggression as "exciting" is an important shift from the more restrictive version of traditional femininity.

## Incompatibilities Between
## Personal and Professional Roles

We asked our experts how the commitments, responsibilities, or expectations of being a psychotherapist interfere with satisfying relationships with significant others in their lives. Table 4.5 shows the scoring of responses.

Over two-thirds of the respondents identified a variety of ways in which their profession as psychotherapists interfered with satisfying relationships with significant others in their lives. Many talked about feeling drained emotionally by the intensity of their work with clients — the need to be present and empathic

Table 4.5. Personal and Professional Role Conflicts.

---

"How does being a therapist get in the way of satisfying relationships with husband, children, parents, friends?"

| | *Responses (%)* |
|---|---|
| Drains energy and time that could be spent with family, friends; increases need/desire to be alone | 53 |
| Therapist for family—either expected to solve family's problems or resented for "playing therapist" with family | 12 |
| Response includes both of the above | 4 |
| Response states there is no interference between roles | 31 |

---

when clients are experiencing and expressing what can be debilitating emotional trauma and helplessness. The psychotherapist's responsibilty to a dependent and disabled client can require the therapist to be "on call" for extended periods of time. These situations can leave them feeling a strong need for quiet and aloneness when they are away from their work, which can stir up resentment from friends and family members. Comments from the respondents best illustrate the conflict and how they experience it.

From a mother of three children: "With all the above people [husband, children, parents, friends], there is some resentment about not having 'more' of me when they want it—especially children—and there is *my* conflict over not being more available."

The conflict is felt by a sixty-year-old wife with no children: "Sometimes one has to put a client's needs ahead of one's relationship with . . . husband and friends. This can lead to anger and rejection, especially if considerable time is involved. One must deal with this problem openly."

A thirty-six-year-old mother of two very young children said, "Sometimes after difficult days, after giving so much attention elsewhere, I want to be selfish and receive more than give, and therefore have less for those most important for me. If this happened too frequently, however, I would reassess what I am doing."

An associate professor of psychiatry responded, "Mostly [the problem is] the time commitment coupled with my need to do what I do well. I'm never done reading or learning and sometimes return home exhausted. I am seldom available for spontaneous fun with friends. I schedule carefully in order to spend long weekends with grown offspring and my grandchildren whom I have worked at knowing on an individual personal basis."

From a single mother of three children:*"I'm tired* and often too drained to hear [my family]! (I'm *very* concerned about this!)"

Having raised six children, this sixty-eight-year-old consultant and professor knows what she needs: "Therapy is intense and relationship-oriented between me and the individual(s) in my office, and I need a lot of peace and quiet to balance this. My husband and I do a lot of quiet things — reading, listening to music, walking, meditating."

Another threat to relationships with significant others is the *satisfaction* that the psychotherapist experiences in her relationships with her clients. One aspect of the work that makes it so rewarding is the opportunity to develop a meaningful relationship with another person, even if that relationship is unequal in terms of the way each person gives and gets. One respondent said that sometimes therapy relationships feel more intimate, more rewarding, and/or more exciting than those with family and friends. "Sometimes the world one projects to patients is so ideal that all others can look like poor copies." The focus in therapy is often so intense that there may not be the trivia or the mundane that our day-to-day contact with husbands and children can consist of: "Relationships with clients are rather dramatic, and sometimes real life is boring by comparison."

Another woman felt her friendships needed to be less intimate and more recreational to prevent burnout. "I'm careful not to overwork because it would be easy for my patients to get the best of me and for me to want to be alone after work. I notice I don't have that much need for closeness left after my patients and family, so [I] have more activity-oriented time with friends and less intense talks than [I] used to have."

Others use their work to avoid burnout in their personal

lives, as the following comment illustrates. "There is always the danger of 'burnout' and that it is easier to have 'intimacy' with patients than to deal with the feelings of your family and to respond and give of yourself. It is easier to be in the office than to respond to the realities of one's personal life."

Ethical standards prohibit dual relationships with clients. Some women commented on the limitations imposed by this concern and occasions when they had to avoid social settings where clients might be. This was expecially so for women in nonurban areas where options for social contacts are more limited. "As a 'single' woman I [was] prohibited from participation in many groups where I would encounter patients." Another woman who was experiencing the isolation in her professional setting said: "It's the only profession I know where friendships with clients are outlawed — so it's limiting."

Another woman expressed concern that to compensate for the isolation, she became "super-independent and probably too competent" to a point where she questioned her capacity for intimacy outside of her therapy clients.

Becoming involved with other people's problems allows one to hide from her own — another interference that the respondents mentioned. Our problems can pale in comparison to others and thus allow us to escape our own problematic relationships. In one woman's words, "[Being a psychotherapist] can lead to a tendency to intellectualize or deny one's own areas of weakness. One can also tend to overdo or overfunction with clients as a way of avoiding self and relationship issues." A divorced mother of two said, "You can get so enthralled with your work — and its intensity — that it takes away from personal relationships — or allows you to hide the truths of a bad relationship."

Family and friends sometimes expect psychotherapists to be "more" for them because they are therapists — more understanding, more available, more tolerant, more insightful. These expectations can feed into the guilt psychotherapists feel when they want, in fact, to retreat from their role as caretaker. It can also play on their need to be the savior: "You end up being too helpful to others and forget how to let others know you also have needs. It becomes hard to limit others' demands on you. The line between therapist and martyr blurs." The flip side of this bind is that friends and families sometimes criticize the psychotherapist for "playing shrink" when she acts in ways that are associated with a therapeutic style. One respondent said that her son complains to his friends, "Other [kids'] mothers yell, mine wants to talk about what I've done."

Nearly one-third of the sample said that being a psychotherapist does *not* interfere. As one family therapist said, "I think, if anything, being a therapist helps [in other relationships]; almost any other profession I can think of would get in the way more. The issues of overcommitment and burnout apply anywhere, and I think, less for a therapist than for others."

However, the potential for interference needs to be recognized: "I don't feel it gets in the way a great deal as long as I have humility! There is a tendency to overanalyze relationships with peers and spouse and try to 'work on them' instead of, at times, riding along with the ups and downs (and adversities) of life. With kids and parents, there is so much emotional voltage that I avoid analyzing as much as possible."

### In a Community of Learners

Lev-El (1983) reviewed research by Douvan (1976) that identified the positive influence of peer support groups and female role models on the development of professional identity in women. We included questions about the extent to which our respondents work and/or trained with other women. Data are presented in Table 4.6. Respondents reported that approximately two-thirds of their clientele were female. This figure is consistent with the number of female clients in general, for both male and female psychotherapists.

The range of time during which our experts received graduate training comprised nearly sixty years, from the late 1920s through the late 1980s. The average was the 1960s. The diplomates, all but thirteen of whom had a doctorate and received their degrees an average of more than twenty-five years ago, reported much lower percentages of female students in their graduate programs and as graduate faculty. Likewise, 24 percent

Table 4.6. Presence of Women as Clients, Colleagues, Trainers.

|  | Diplomates (%) | Family Therapists (%) | Total (%) |
|---|---|---|---|
| Female clients | 65.7 | 67.0 | 66.3 |
| Female students in program | 32.0 | 66.4 | 45.5 |
| Female faculty | 16.9 | 46.8 | 27.8 |
| Female supervisors | 24.0 | 48.0 | 33.6 |
| Female colleagues | 38.9 | 56.5 | 45.8 |

of their clinical supervisors during training and since have been female, and almost 39 percent of their work colleagues are female. For the group of family therapists, many of whom have degrees in social work, females made up two-thirds of the students in their programs and nearly half of the graduate faculty. Close to half of clinical supervisors and more than half of their work colleagues were female. These figures illustrate the significant presence of women in this discipline.

The presence or absence of other females as teachers, classmates, supervisors, or coworkers did not seem to significantly influence career satisfaction. Both groups were highly satisfied with their career choice: on a scale of 1 (very disappointed) to 5 (very satisfied), the average rating was 4.67.

## Coping and Self-Care

While we are struggling to assume a new integrated model of femininity, we can use practical advice for coping with the burdens of our multiple roles. Psychologist Berta Davis (1983) presents four criteria to be considered in managing a career as wife, mother, and therapist. She says that (1) women therapists need to merge their assertive and nurturant selves, (2) the husband-wife relationship needs to take priority over the mother-child or therapist-client relationships, (3) adjustments to work schedules need to be made as needs of children change, and (4) husbands need to be supportive of their wives' careers by sharing child-rearing and homemaking responsibilities. The husband-wife relationship is especially important in lessening the risk of using therapeutic relationships to satisfy intimacy needs. Davis believes that the mother and therapist roles are more secure if one's "primary allegiance [is] to one's mate" (p. 19). Davis (1983) and McGoldrick (1987) both discuss the value of employing someone to take over routine domestic duties (cleaning, shopping, meal preparation) to free up more energy for relationships with the family, as well as energy for pursuing one's career.

Coleman and Kaplan's (1987) advice focuses on the self of the therapist and includes reflecting on our own needs that are not being met by either family or career and making an "honest self-exploration of our career goals and needs" (pp. 75–76). They advocate choosing a self-nurturing "third environment," such as a physical activity or creative interest, that provides a contrast with our career and family responsibilities and is not emotionally taxing. "It is therapeutic to have at least one segment of her life that does not demand that she give, listen, or problem-solve . . . [that provides] freedom from expectations of others" (p. 75). They also encourage fun time with the family. The authors acknowledge the extra time demands implied by engaging in such self-reflection and exploring a "third environment" and that many women will resist giving to themselves until they have met the needs of others. But, because it is so similar to the advice we give to our clients and our friends, we know the wisdom of it. Taking care of ourselves is a prerequisite for caring for others.

## Using Mutuality of Relationships as Balance

The majority of our experts have recognized and employed mutuality in their relationships both in work and personal life. They have used with clients what has worked for them in nurturing others — children, aging parents, friends, lovers. Their training in tolerance and in accepting limitations — their own and others — is invaluable to them in all their roles. Those who manage to juggle responsibilities and identities effectively do so because they are flexible and adaptable and have found continuity in their experiences. Their comments reflect this remarkable reciprocity of love and work at its best.

A sixty-year-old retired diplomate who raised three children commented, "I became a better mother because I finally began to practice what I preached [to clients] especially in regard to setting limits, feeling less guilty and responsible for my children's behavior (less need to accept responsibility and control). I also learned to take care of myself and my primary relationship (marriage) *first.*"

"I see myself and myself with spouse reflected in my clients' interactions. My process of working with them is very much one of continuing to learn about myself and to experiment with new solutions, ways of seeing the world that I can apply to my own life." This comment comes from a forty-two-year-old family therapist.

A daughter improved a relationship with her mother who had Alzheimer's disease by using skills developed in therapy: "When I began to talk with her, and listen, and enjoy the exchange of the moment, . . . our time together once again became mutually pleasurable."

The women drew strength and hope from witnessing their clients' dilemmas: "Sometimes I marvel at how clients persevere. It's enabling. Frustrations involved in handling a number of responsibilities (wife, mother, dying parents, homemaker, family-entertainment chairperson, etc.) took on a different perspective based on what some clients endured."

From a diplomate on the West coast: "My clients work things out in ways I could not have imagined for them. They take steps towards independence that I would have feared to urge on them — but gladly support them when they do. This gives me faith that my daughters, too, will find their ways through the maze."

In Chapter Two, we described Constructed Knowers, a category posited by Belenky and her colleagues (1986), as respecting the wisdom gained from self-awareness, personal experience, and intuition. They use this wisdom to make a difference in the lives of others. We hear a constructivist's voice from a woman who cared for a dying friend: "My closest friend died of cancer three years ago. Because of my understanding of my own fears and feelings, I was able to comfort her and connect with her throughout her illness, and not abandon her."

Another woman applies her self-awareness to improve her relationships with others: "I've learned a great deal about the process of relationships—the ups, downs, the ways that my family issues get recreated, the limits of relationship, the damaging effects of negative projections, and the failure to be self-focused. I try to be engaged with my spouse just as I would [with] a client—with empathy, nurturing, and honest self-examination."

Lessons in personal and professional relationships are mutually enriching, as the following comments illustrate.

From an administrator of a private hospital mental health clinic: "I've been happily married for thirty-seven years. What I have learned from that is that as long as both partners think of giving to the other, just a bit more than about what they want to get, the relationship thrives. That means focusing just a bit more on being sensitive and considerate than on one's own needs. In my work with couples, I try to impart that information. It is useful for a therapist to have a focus on the other more than on self. I give my husband my attempt to listen objectively to what he is trying to communicate."

A specialist in working with stepfamilies responded, "To me it seems the other way round—what I learned in working with people has been useful in my spousal relationship. Becoming a therapist propelled me into self-examination and needed emotional learning that produced difficulties in my first marriage— and has really been positive in my second."

The importance of reciprocity is clear in this family therapist's remarks: "It takes an ability to give to another as one would want a person to give to you, . . . it involves trust, struggle, independence, dependence, being grounded, ambivalence, and ability to be flexible. What I give to my clients that is similar to what I give to a friend/spouse is the recognition and sense of comfortableness that all of the above is part of a committed relationship."

Many of the women write that the process that occurs in their relationships with friends and spouses bears similarity to the process with clients. They refer repeatedly to the art of listening as an expression of love, the rewards of accepting others rather than expecting them to change, and the willingness to work on relationships through their inevitable ups and downs.

They acknowledge that they gain from their relationships with clients through greater self-understanding and self-acceptance. Many of them comment on being deeply touched by clients who illustrate again and again the power of human potential yet the frailty of the human condition — the paradox of the strength derived from being vulnerable:

"They taught me so much. I love being a therapist because of the intimacy and opportunity to know so many fine people who let me learn from their lives about different cultural values, new ways to see the world, new ways to cope, and the fact that we can all change, if we want to."

The mutuality of these relationships replenishes them and is woven into the fabric of their identities. As Mary Catherine Bateson says, "each of us has discovered, in spite of double-shift labor and competing demands, that we are nurtured by our work and that we can combine different kinds of tasks so they feed each other — mostly — instead of competing" (p. 238).

The lives of women therapists reflect the interdependence of love and work as they carry out the tasks of the lover, friend, clinician, mother, researcher, daughter, and teacher.

# 5

## The Obstacle Course
## to Success

*I said, "Dr. X, you really don't mean that. You would never
ask a man to do that," and smiled sweetly. He backed off.*
— Anonymous

The concept of the "glass ceiling" refers to the invisible barrier
that prevents women and minorities from reaching the highest
levels of career achievement. For female professionals in many
fields, the highest level to which they can realistically aspire is
somewhere below what their white male colleagues can expect
to achieve. The frustration is in the *apparent* transparency of the
barrier—women and minorities have been encouraged to believe that the opportunities are equal for all individuals within
a given profession who have comparable training and experience. But the statistics show that the glass ceiling is an impene-
trable barrier for many women and minorities. Unable to climb
the predictable career ladder, some professionals have found
themselves on an obstacle course confronted by traps, inaccurate
maps, and occasional landmines.

Attitudes of sexism and racism, prejudice, and stereotyp-
ing have created this glass ceiling. Bernice Lott (1985) provided
an extensive review of studies on the ways in which women who
are equal in ability and performance to men are evaluated as
being less competent. Men tend to devalue the competency of

women more consistently than women devalue women. Even women who are more competent than men will be seen as less competent in many situations. Furthermore, evaluations will be more consistently negative for women when the context involves a potential hiring or promoting decision rather than simply evaluating credentials or performance. The implications of these studies are that gender is an obstacle for women aspiring to successful careers.

The evidence provided by salary statistics and the paucity of women in managerial or executive positions reveals that women, as a group, have advanced very little in terms of equality in employment opportunities since the women's movement began in the early 1970s. Susan Faludi (1991) counters the argument that women have made strides in attaining equal rights in all areas of our society. The vast majority of working women continue to be employed in "pink collar" jobs as secretaries and waitresses and to be discriminated against and sexually harassed. She attacks antifeminists who insist that women are receiving fair treatment, wages, and opportunities. Faludi says, "The truth is that the last decade has been a powerful counterassault on women's rights, a backlash, an attempt to retract the handful of small and hard-won victories that the feminist movement did manage to win for women" (xvii).

Surveys on income and employment status of psychologists conducted by the American Psychological Association (Cohen and Gutek, 1991) show that men earn more money than women and are more likely to be employed full-time. Likewise, faculty members from graduate programs are more helpful to male students in job placement and more likely to develop personal relationships with them. Women are more likely to have to choose between career and personal lives, as indicated by Cohen and Gutek:

- When forced to relocate to assume a better job, over 96 percent of the men's partners moved with them while barely two-thirds of the women's partners moved.
- For those professionals who were neither working nor seeking employment, family and home responsibilities were cited as the reason by over 50 percent of the women but by fewer than 5 percent of the men.

Many of the women psychotherapists in our sample found the path to success complex and circuitous. In this chapter, we will look at how these women maneuvered their way along the obstacle course to success. They will share the hardships they faced from gender discrimination as well as how they responded to being given lower salaries and less influential positions. They tell us how they dealt with sexual harassment. They reveal how their own self-esteem sometimes provided an unwitting obstacle to success. They identify what they believe to be their own strategies for competing successfully.

Even their own families presented some problems, as we saw in Chapter Four. Although parents may have expressed pride in their daughters' achievements, they were often fearful that having a career would interfere with their primary goal for their daughter of having a family. The following comment represents this position. "[My parents] would have approved more of marriage and children. My professional achievement and success remains, to a degree, an enigma [to them]."

Those experts who began their education and career after marriage apparently fared better than some who married after their careers were established or never married. Our respondents frequently reported that their husbands were quite supportive and served as role models and even mentors.

Their socialization as females presented its own set of obstacles. Our experts had to unlearn early behaviors such as being passive, fearful, doing for others, rescuing, and enabling. A major obstacle for many women psychotherapists was their lack of awareness and acceptance of their power. Said one woman, "I received mixed messages about power. Some messages said women may be powerful, 'but don't overpower men.' The first message was very helpful. The second message was totally useless." Such mixed messages may account for the ambivalence of some of the women in our sample about perceiving themselves as powerful, as we discussed in Chapter Three. Societal standards encourage women to be powerful in some situations but not in others. Traditionally women are encouraged to be subordinate in male-dominated situations, such as the world of work. This message is a major obstacle for women aspiring to successful careers, especially in male-dominated fields.

Acknowledging the influence of socialization, McGoldrick, Anderson, and Walsh (1989) state, "Two stereotypic female characteristics, empathy and a relational focus, work for the female therapist, while a third, passivity, works against positive outcome. Female therapists are advised to take an active role and to develop a style that helps them to deal with power effectively" (p. 163). We will talk more about how women can overcome these counterproductive influences later in this chapter. Bateson (1989) identified "two kinds of vulnerability that women raised in our society tend to have. . . . The first is the quality of self-sacrifice, a learned willingness to set their own interests aside and be used and even used up by the community. . . . The second . . . is a readiness to believe messages of disdain and derogation" (p. 54). The women in our sample seem to have unlearned the message that they are expected to be self-sacrificing. We hear much self-confidence in their voices. The success and satisfaction they have experienced in their careers has apparently been affirming.

The greatest barrier experienced by our women psychotherapists was discrimination. This occurred in a variety of forms. For example, access to education was affected when women were denied graduate school admissions because, they were told, they were taking a place a man should have. By their reports, women were not given scholarships or assistantships and were granted less financial support for their education than their male colleagues. Women had less access to mentors who could further their careers, a point we will discuss in greater depth in Chapter Six. After they had completed their degrees, discrimination continued to affect their careers when they were hired for lower status positions and at lower salaries. Our women also report examples of sexual harassment and emotional abuse.

The amount of damage caused by discrimination was moderate in most cases, but these are the reports of women who stayed in the profession and succeeded. Those who were more severely damaged may have left to pursue other careers and thus are not represented in the sample. Several of the women said they did not feel they had experienced discrimination. A few even reported that their gender gave them an advantage in their access to career advancement. Some women seem to have taken for granted that they would experience discrimination and even found a way to rationalize it. For example, a sixty-one-year-old teacher, trainer, and private clinician said, "None of [my experiences with discrimination] have been other than the garden variety. I have often been a token woman and benefited from that."

Reactions to being discriminated against varied widely. Some women ignored it, kept quiet, or accepted it, sometimes out of fear of further retribution. Others confronted the situation or the offender either verbally or by filing a grievance or bringing suit. Still others used their experience to guide others in addressing discrimination more effectively. A professor of psychology in a Boston university said, "In response to a lifetime of discrimination, I developed several courses on the psychology of women [and] serve on harassment and ethics committees. I take it as my responsibility to help psychologists who are getting hurt by such discrimination." Another woman, who did not confront her offender decades ago, has attempted to compensate for her lack of action at the time: "A world-famous psychologist and mentor tried to seduce me. I did nothing then — I was only twenty-five. Since then, I've helped younger women fight this kind of insult from supervisors and therapists. There was no sanction against this twenty-five years ago." Table 5.1 presents the data on the amount of damage from the incident as perceived by our respondents and the methods of conflict resolution they used.

## Educational Discrimination

Many of the women therapists were attending graduate school prior to the 1970s, and attitudes toward women students were overtly discriminatory. Women and minorities often have had to "work harder" to be taken seriously as professionals. A woman states, "A professor in graduate school recommended I should quit, marry, and have a family. My response was to work harder and hang in there."

A woman's commitment to her education and career is more likely to be doubted, especially if she is married and/or

### Table 5.1. Effects of Gender Discrimination.

"Are you aware of gender discrimination levied against you? If so, describe the worst incident. What action plan did you take in response? What action plan did you consider but not take?"

| *Amount of Damage* | *Responses (%)* |
|---|---|
| No damage — Respondent states the incident was harmless. ("I was none the worse for wear.") | 41 |
| Some damage — Respondent states some degree of negative aftereffect. ("I managed even though I earned less than the males.") | 45 |
| Severe damage — Respondent says that career was negatively altered as a result. ("I gave up my goal of a career in academia after that.") | 14 |
| *Method of Conflict Resolution* | |
| Leave the scene — Respondent withdrew, emotionally or physically. ("I got a different job." "I ignored it.") | 55 |
| Direct confrontation — Public address of issue ("I filed a grievance." "I confronted my boss.") | 37 |
| Confront later or help others — Respondent waited, then confronted directly or helped other women confront such issues. ("I developed workshops on dealing with gender discrimination.") | 6 |
| Leave, then confront — Respondent left the job or the graduate program, then filed a suit or complaint. | 2 |

attractive. One woman says, "When I applied to graduate school in '68, I was asked to write a letter that I would stay three years, but my husband [also a graduate student] was not asked to write any such promise. It was explained to me that many women had left with their husbands before finishing their degrees. I complied. I don't think this would happen now."

Educational discrimination also comes in the form of access to financial support. The Boston professor quoted earlier also stated, "I was the only one of five entering students in my graduate class at Yale not offered a scholarship, even though I was at least competitive with the others, all males." Another woman kept her fellowship after confronting her director: "I was asked by [the] director to give up my fellowship for another student because my husband had [a] good job. I said, 'Dr. X, you don't really mean that. You would never ask a man to do that,' and smiled sweetly. He backed off."

Several of our respondents found that their institutions were unwilling to invest money in the education of women when the woman's commitment was in question, no matter how much promise she showed.

## Job Discrimination

Institutions of higher education continued to discriminate against some of the women respondents when they moved from the role of student to that of professor. In fact, of various kinds of work settings identified in examples of discriminatory treatment, colleges and universities were mentioned with greater frequency than any other institution. Women in our sample who worked in higher education attributed failure to be promoted, receive raises, or even be hired to gender discrimination in their institutions. The following examples illustrate these practices.

A now-retired diplomate reported, "The worst time was during [the] time I taught at [a] university. It was obvious because I was female [that] I would not get my associate professorship and would not get monetary rewards or tenure like my male colleagues. That's why I left and went into [the] clinical field. It was particularly bad in [the] '40s and '50s. Some universities had quotas for female staff."

Another retired and unmarried diplomate stated, "Early on in my teaching career, I was told by my boss that he couldn't give me a raise that year because another young faculty member (male) needed it more, since he was married and his wife had just had a baby. I didn't take any action in reprisal, but it's also true that I left that teaching post in the next couple of years, but not as a direct response to the discrimination."

Being married was a basis for discrimination, as the following woman reported: "About seven years ago, I discovered that the female professors were all earning several thousand dollars per year less than males of equal rank, experience, etc. I confronted the Dean, unsuccessfully. I was actually told that since

I was married and 'supported by my husband,' it was fair. I did not pursue [it] further, and I should have."

Another woman's career plans were altered because of discriminatory treatment: "Many instances of discrimination. The worst was that no psychology department would hire a woman in 1957. This forever foreclosed me from a research career."

Current figures reveal that women comprise only 27 percent of the faculties in colleges and universities. Only 10 percent of all full professors are women (Sagaria, 1988). According to Sandler (1986), "On the average, colleges and universities nationwide employ only 1.1 senior woman (dean and above) per institution" (p. 14). Percentages of female administrators are similar to those of female faculty, with the majority of female administrators being at middle-management or staff levels. Salary levels of female faculty are 9 percent lower than those of male faculty of comparable rank; female administrators' salaries are 15 percent lower than those of male administrators in comparable positions with comparable levels of experience. (Faculty salary information was calculated based on data reported in *Academe*, Bulletin of the American Association of University Professors, 1992, *78* (2), p. 20. Administrative salary information was calculated based on data provided by College and University Personnel Association, Washington, D.C., 1991–1992.)

## Women's Work

A second form of job discrimination includes ways in which women are not given credit or recognition for their work and are encouraged to choose arenas for practice that are stereotypic.

From a clinician who began her career after her six children were born: "I was told when I first started practice (sixteen years ago) that I'd have a better chance of success if I chose to work with children, and that men would not come to see a woman. I did not want to work with children [and] now restrict my practice to adults and some older teenagers and work well with both genders."

Women in the helping professions may be more vulnerable to discrimination than women in other professions because they are viewed as doing what women do naturally, that is, nurture. These same nurturing traits may be played upon when women are expected to settle for less pay and recognition in deference to their male colleagues, as we see in the two comments that follow.

Even though she was an unmarried career woman, one respondent "was asked to allow males to take credit for my work because it was 'more important for their career' (in the late '60s, early '70s)."

Women are sometimes penalized for taking time out for new babies, as one woman reported: "I completed my part of a grant proposal . . . at the same time I was having my second child and proceeded to stay at home with [the] new baby for six weeks. [The] grant was submitted and when I saw [the] final version that was approved for funding, I saw a male as the co-principal investigator, not me. I resigned and started full[-time] in private practice. One and a half years later, they begged me to return [saying], 'since you left nothing creative has come out of here.'"

Women employers also have contributed to discrimination by expecting that women will be paid lower salaries. One diplomate reported, "My first Ph.D. level position was offered to me by a woman who would have been my supervisor, at an embarrassingly low salary, with the comment that, since I was married, the salary was irrelevant. I did not take the job; no further pursuit of her outrageous behavior occurred to me at the time."

Another diplomate experienced similar attitudes in her co-workers. "In my first job . . . most female therapists (psychologists and social workers) were married females. I was [the] sole support of three children and felt [my colleagues'] resistance to pressing for better salaries. They were content with 'easy' jobs and low pay. The security was most important to them. I began to develop a private practice and left within two years."

Many women in the mental health field can make career changes without having to leave the profession. Going into private practice is one way that women have coped with mistreatment within the institution. Other avenues for resolving their conflicts included consideration of or actual confrontation, as in the following examples.

A medical school professor reported, "I was earning $9,000 per year when all [my] male colleagues were earning $16,000 or more. I filed a class action suit for discrimination against women and received a $7,000 raise. Alternately, my chairman called me a 'hostile, aggressive, castrating bitch' on three occasions, all in private. I considered bringing a grievance procedure but felt that no good would result, so I took no action."

From a family therapist now in private practice, "I filed an EEOC and Labor Department complaint against a community mental health center for differential pay and promotion. Both complaints were upheld, but EEOC could not force the county to give back pay—this was in [the] late '70s."

All too often, women try to correct for injustices by working harder. "As [the] only female (chair, too) of [an] all-male academic department, I was sabotaged and undermined. I confronted it directly—considered legal action but did not do that. [Instead, I] overfunctioned and overachieved!"

Another frequent coping strategy is to move on to another setting. From a diplomate in higher education administration, "I did not get serious consideration for the vice president position in my present institution. Subsequently [a] white male vice president [was] hired [who] doesn't like my style. [I am] too direct and intimidating to him. I considered filing a discrimination complaint; instead I'm looking for a new job."

Even in victory, there is defeat: "After several years as director of pupil services and the only woman on [the] administrative council, the male members met one evening without informing me—at a period of budget cuts—and eliminated the position. Protests were made mostly by my fellow psychologists, in the newspapers, etc. Eventually they created a position for me—program evaluation, but I lost both status and money."

Emotional losses are also deeply felt: "At one point I had to file a gender discrimination suit since the men were trying to get rid of me. When I won the suit, the response by the men was to comment about a woman at another hospital who also won a suit: 'She was just a whore anyway' was their comment."

## Covert Gender Discrimination

The unfair actions of others are often more covert than overt. This form of discrimination is subtle and is based on expectations that women will be accommodating and work hard to please others on the job. Often women report not being taken seriously as professionals and being disadvantaged because of a lack of understanding about the multiple roles they must serve. Although the most blatant forms of discrimination involved sexual harassment, the less direct forms of being overlooked and undervalued were reported. The following comment is typical of more subtle forms of sexual harassment: "The other sexual discrimination I have experienced has been more or less subtle, for instance, being mistaken for a secretary, comments about my clothes or figure, and the assumption that I didn't *have* to make a living."

A diplomate who teaches at an Eastern university reported, "Before I was scheduled to take my diplomate exam, the local administrator called me. He told me he was happy for me that I was taking my exam because my husband was so well known in the field that it would be good for me to have my own reputation. I was flabbergasted, since I was already teaching and publishing and had a successful practice. He went on to say that he was especially attuned to this problem, since *his* wife was in his field as well. I am still outraged whenever I think about the incident."

The words of one diplomate illustrate the expectation that women not be too competent, not attract attention to their skills. "[The] worst incident [was] when I was not permitted to do something innovative; I was expected to be quietly compliant and never rock the boat. [The] power structure was patriarchal at the time. I continued to advocate my ideas. . . . When [the] power structure changed, I was given carte blanche to pursue my ideas."

The following comment from a director of family services best captures the frustration of these forms of discrimination: "I don't think women are ever listened to as seriously as men, even by men who try not to be chauvinistic. This does not take the form of outrageous incidents, but it is always there, like a nagging toothache."

Women have recently gained greater recourse for action against more blatant forms of discrimination, thanks to affirmative action laws, ethics committees, and sexual harassment policies. Despite the forms of protection that exist, discrimination has only been partly deterred. This form of prejudice continues to keep its victims in a two-down position. Not only do they suffer from inequality in treatment, but they also have the burden of proving the violation. As reported by some of our respondents, even if they win the decision, they may lose the spirit of collegiality that is often so important to one's sense of well-being in the workplace.

## Tools for Competing Successfully

Despite the obstacles of gender and financial discrimination, the majority of our women psychotherapists view themselves as having successfully competed in a highly competitive professional domain. They attribute their accomplishment to their competence as clinicians and to personal qualities such as self-awareness, trustworthiness, intelligence, and ambition. Table 5.2 represents these results.

Self-confidence both contributes to one's feeling of success and is derived from evidence of one's success. The voices of the respondents were filled with self-confidence. From a family

**Table 5.2. Competing Successfully.**

"What qualities or skills that you possess are most helpful to you in competing successfully in the highly competitive field of psychology?"

|  | Responses (%) |
|---|---|
| Competence — Respondent mentions being skilled in her trade, being goal-directed, persistent, hardworking. | 21 |
| Personal qualities — Respondent mentions interpersonal skills, self-confidence, self-awareness, intelligence, ability to empathize, being emotionally centered. | 32 |
| Both competence and personal qualities are mentioned. | 47 |

therapist, "I am intelligent, insightful, committed, and caring. It is easy for me to tolerate ambivalence and to see issues from several viewpoints." A diplomate listed: "Self-confidence, aggressiveness, competence . . . in short, being good at my work, knowing that and being comfortable communicating it."

These women are not afraid to work hard. They often attribute their success to their persistence, which, in combination with personal qualities, has contributed to their skillfulness. Simply put by one of our respondents, success comes from "perseverance and guts." A woman who has published two books says it takes, "tenaciousness, brightness, aggressivity when needed, interpersonal skill, hard work, a capacity to learn from my and others' talents and mistakes, and ambition to make a central contribution."

Only 13 percent of the respondents felt that they had not competed successfully or said they did not see themselves as competitive.

Women from earlier generations were taught that competition was unfeminine, that their success was threatening to others and would alienate them from others. In *My Mother/My Self* (1977), Nancy Friday says, "An important step has been left out of our socialization: Mother raises us to win people's love. She gives us no training in the emotions of rivalry that would lose it for us. With no practical experience in the rules that make competition safe, we fear its ferocity. Never having been taught to win, we do not know how to lose" (p. 166). The "fear of success" can be all too real, as evidenced in the following comment from a woman who avoids competition: "I try not to directly compete. I attempt to be competent, but whenever I have been competitive I have suffered unforunate results. I am not good at power struggles. I will always try to do the best job that I know how. This is sometimes successful, and sometimes it is not successful." It is not surprising that we fear that which we do not see ourselves as having under control, when even doing the best job that we know how is no assurance of success. Women have had to overcome the covert discrimination of society's expectations and their own self-image, as well as overt discrimination.

## Caring and Competition

Many women psychotherapists view the personal qualities of caring and the skills of interpersonal communication as crucial to their effectiveness as therapists. In Chapter Three, we saw that the respondents ranked empathy and interpersonal skills as very important to effective psychotherapy. They frequently identify their competence in these areas as accounting for their success. For example, one woman cites her "good understanding of people and emotions, sincere concern and compassion, integrity and adherence to higher values, good intervention/ therapeutic skills." Effective interpersonal communication skills and empathic caring allow these women to be genuine and nonthreatening to their clients, qualities that engender trust in the therapy relationship. The following comments illustrate these qualities.

Genuineness and authenticity engender trust: "I'm a natural person—comfortable talking about anything—have a range of deep feelings myself—not afraid of intimacy or responsibility for people. Patients feel they can put themselves in my hands as therapy gets tough."

Support and understanding are valued: "Ability to empathize, ability to recognize patient vulnerability and not make it so scary, provide a safe, trusting relationship."

A teacher and trainer recognizes the importance of role modeling: "Ability to connect with my clients. The ability to be relevant to my clients. The ability to give my clients a model of functioning they can *use.*"

## Overcoming Obstacles

Some of the respondents referred to having to overcome obstacles in order to allow themselves to compete and be successful. Those obstacles may be what contributed to the small percentage of women who seemed to have a negative concept of competition or, at least, of themselves as competing successfully. The qualities of humility and attractiveness are perceived as barriers in the following comment from a director of a guidance center:

"I am reasonably bright, articulate, good-humored, confident in myself, willing to try new things, well-grounded ethically, straight in communications, firm, physically attractive enough to be noticed but not overwhelming, appreciative of others' skills/knowledge, willing to learn *and* willing to ignore, *and* not be troubled by an overactive sense of humility." This comment suggests that being *too* attractive detracts from a woman's success but being "attractive enough" adds to it. Women who have experienced sexual harassment or have been victims of sexual assault sometimes cite their physical attractiveness as a cause of the disrespect. Women need to untangle severely mixed messages. "Dressing for success" and conforming to the media image of feminine attractiveness seem to be in contradiction with warnings of how their physical attractiveness can detract from being taken seriously as competent, intelligent professionals.

Another obstacle to success can be a woman's need to please and appease others. This need for "social approval and acceptance" in women is positively correlated with the need to achieve, according to Susan Sandel (1987). She says, "Conversely, men with high achievement needs are explicitly unconcerned with making friends. Thus, they are more likely than women to make tough decisions with a clear conscience and no regrets. The role of the empathic, nurturing, and creative clinician is more compatible with affiliative needs than that of administrator/decision maker" (p. 110). The following quotation from one of our experts identifies this conflict: "I am competitive about achieving goals once I establish them. I am willing to stick to decisions or to a course even when this might meet with negative reactions. Women often render themselves unable to pursue their goals because of their strong need for approval." A different interpretation is that women may choose to change their goals when they are in conflict with their relationships. Either way—whether by deliberate choice or acquiescence for the sake of earning approval—their career goals are altered. Once again, we see women being (or perceiving themselves to be) in the position of choosing *between* roles rather than making choices that allow them to coordinate multiple roles.

But most of the women psychotherapists seem to coordinate multiple roles and seem to have achieved the self-confidence they see as so critical to being successful. As one family therapist from our sample said: "Self-confidence is most helpful and has taken a long time to build in a male-dominated discipline. *Willingness* to compete, to disagree, to take a stance and test it, receive challenges and consider them, challenge back — these are skills that were de-emphasized in my socialization but were very important in my success."

### The Struggle to Put Oneself First — Claudia Bepko

Claudia Bepko has been extremely successful both as a writer and as a practicing family therapist. She is respected and admired for her dedication in the treatment of alcoholism from a family systems model and in her inspiring ability to help women become more assertive in taking care of their own needs. Unlike many of the women who answered this questionnaire, Claudia Bepko received her professional training in an environment that was primarily composed of females. She reports that she was able to circumvent gender discrimination in institutions. "I have not directly experienced a great deal of specific discrimination against me. I am much more aware of larger systems issues: the ongoing devaluation and oppression of women. For the most part, I have structured my life outside the direct range of male power or influence." She states that as a feminist, she has been most concerned about women's issues, and yet it's also true that "I have had a great deal of support from men." In academia, she believes that it is typical that a male often mentors female students, because there are fewer female professors and because the female is in a less powerful position as a student and as a woman. Bepko had a male advisor/field instructor when she was in social work training at Rutgers University. Another male professor accused her of plagiarism because "he thought the work I did was too good to have been done by a student." Claudia Bepko learned to stay out of situations where she thought she would be taken advantage of or unfairly treated.

In recounting the path that led her to success, Claudia

Bepko gave a good deal of credit to Monica McGoldrick, a family psychotherapist who has contributed to the development of the use of the genogram in family therapy. Monica McGoldrick helped Claudia and her partner, Jo-Ann Krestan, to edit their first paper. "She spent hours on the phone helping us to finally get the work accepted by *Family Process,*" a major journal in family psychotherapy.

When one sees Claudia's name on two major books, it is difficult to understand how much of an obstacle course she has maneuvered. Claudia and Jo-Ann are coauthors of *The Responsibility Trap: A Blueprint for Treating the Alcoholic Family.* They went on to write *Too Good for Her Own Good,* a discussion of women's tendency to put themselves last. Claudia has two master's degrees, one in literature and another in social work. She recounts how she stumbled into the field of social work. "I wanted to go on for a Ph.D. in English, but the jobs dried up. I changed course because I thought I needed to do what could help me to make a living." Claudia began writing in 1983. She attributes a good deal of her success to her partnership with Jo-Ann Krestan. "Jo-Ann and I have mentored one another. There is a synergy between us. Someone has to be able to be very visible and out there—Jo-Ann does that. The field of family therapy puts emphasis on drama and presentation. You have to be able to get your point across and move an audience—Jo-Ann is good at that."

Claudia's view of her own road to success is that she shares credit with a number of people who have supported her over the years. "Success is never a single event—it always comes with the support and input of others. It is a collaborative venture. Men have been more invested in seeing themselves as conquering heroes, but this is not the way success happens." Claudia Bepko's road map to success indicates that her way of knowing about reality is very similar to the collaborative approach that is so typical of females.

She summarizes: "My obstacles to success have been mainly internal ones. The act of getting myself to write a book took many struggles. I said that I wanted to write, but I didn't know what to write about. I sat down with my friends, who told me to write about what I knew." Claudia Bepko has written and practices what she knows with great success. She has maneuvered the success obstacle course with integrity and with an approach to leadership that is representative of the way women succeed.

## Implications for Career Building

To build a career both women and men need to be prepared to deal with obstacles. Success depends in part on knowing which obstacles to anticipate and devising strategies for avoiding or confronting them without being defeated. The experiences shared by the women in our sample provide guidance to this end.

There are now laws, policies, and ethical standards to protect professionals from blatant forms of discrimination and to provide them with means of recourse when mistreatment occurs. Many of the women in our sample did not have affirmative action policies, review boards or ethics committees, or equal employment laws to protect their rights decades ago. Those women found various ways to protect themselves from discriminatory treatment or to seek justice for damages incurred, as we have seen. In some cases, they directly confronted those responsible for the injustice. These confrontations included registering their awareness of the mistreatment with the individual responsible, as well as demanding that the injustice be rectified. In other cases, they learned their lesson and taught it to others who were entering the profession. In still other cases, they remained silent and either eventually left the environment that they experienced as hostile or chose to stay and protect themselves against future incidents through their own caution. The real protection of our rights cannot be assured until women and men are informed of the laws and policies that protect them and are aware of what treatment constitutes a violation of their rights.

Many of the diplomates and family therapists in our sample learned that they needed to be alert to indications of discrimination based on gender, race, age, and sexual orientation as they built their careers. They needed to seek out mentors and role models who genuinely supported their careers and encouraged their choices. They needed to value their power and recognize that there is strength in the "feminine" qualities of intuition, caring, and responsibility toward others, as well as in the "masculine" qualities of competition, assertiveness, and ambition. We all need both sets for success.

Our women psychotherapists state that self-confidence and competence were fundamental to their success. Other people can know we are good at what we do only if *we* know it. These women have been willing and able to work hard to get the rewards due them. Thus, they diligently pursued training and experience that increased their competence and enhanced their self-confidence.

Braiker (1986, p. 129) says that women need to overcome the fear of success or what she calls "excellence anxiety." "Confusion or fears regarding achievement can make women construct unnecessarily difficult psychological hurdles on their way up the career ladder that make the actual pursuit of success more stressful." Rather than have a need for affiliation and approval of others conflict with their need to achieve, women can employ their relational skills of empathy and intuitiveness toward the achievement of recognition as accomplished professionals.

Bernice Sandler (1986) discusses the need for women to know how to respond to biased behavior and attitudes. Even on an individual basis, women can reduce differential treatment by taking a proactive stance. She recommends such things as claiming your own accomplishment, like a promotion or completion of a piece of research, rather than attributing it to "luck" or "just hard work." She advocates publicly confronting sexist treatment as well as publicly praising nonsexist treatment. Sandler encourages women to refuse to tolerate inappropriate treatment such as sexist humor or stereotyped ideas about women's roles.

As we have heard from their experiences, many of our women have been willing to compete, to take risks, to win, and to lose in order to make the statement that their work, their ideas are a contribution to others and worthy of being shared. Bateson describes the glass ceiling problem in terms of the threat some men feel from women: "Women rise as long as there is a layer of more powerful men above them, whose sense of appropriate relationships is not threatened by the women's aspirations" (1989, p. 107). According to Hymowitz and Schellhardt, "The biggest obstacle women face [in advancement] is also the most intangible. Men . . . feel uncomfortable with women beside them [on the same level]" (1986, p. 1). As men continue to work alongside women, discriminatory attitudes may change. Lott (1985) reviewed studies that show that when evaluators have actual experience with a competent woman, they will more readily acknowledge her capabilities than if they are personally unfamiliar with the woman.

## Gender and Leadership Styles

Controversy continues to surround the research on gender differences in leadership and management styles. Although male and female managers do not differ significantly in terms of personality characteristics and managerial abilities, women still believe that they need to outperform men in order to gain credibility (Morrison, White, and Van Velsor, 1987). According to McGoldrick, Anderson, and Walsh (1989), female psychotherapists have a harder time establishing themselves as authority figures than men because women are expected to be supportive. The authors say, "our culture continues to grant males superior status . . . and since females expect to have less authority and less status . . . , stereotypes continue to downgrade female competence and authority. Competent women tend to be seen as sex-role incongruent . . . ; other traits associated with effectiveness and competence (e.g. assertiveness and competitiveness) are seen as inappropriate for women" (p. 157).

As we mentioned earlier in this chapter, the conflict between the need to achieve and the need for affiliation interferes with women's desire to seek positions of authority. Women do not want to experience the alienation that is associated with those in power. "The person may be warm and understanding, but as an authority may at times be viewed as punitive, unconcerned, and all the other negative qualities that we attribute to our boss" (Sandel, 1987, p. 110). Competent women can combat excellence anxiety and learn how to exercise power and authority in ways that are compatible with their affiliative needs. Women managers can learn to avoid behaviors that are both traditionally feminine (for example, passive and emotional) and masculine (for example, dominant and autocratic). They can increase their awareness that bosses and co-workers may have distorted stereotypes about women in management. Many of our experts serve as examples that women can be extremely competent, forceful, and task-oriented while employing a collaborative management style. This style enhances cooperative relationships among co-workers, which are referred to as maintenance behaviors (encouraging, supporting).

Alice Eagly and colleagues (DeAngelis, 1991) examined the literature on gender differences in leadership styles and reached the following conclusions:

- In general, women leaders/managers are more democratic than autocratic and are more concerned with group morale and interpersonal relationships.
- When the task is relatively "feminine" (for example, counseling, nursing), women are as task-oriented as men.
- Women leaders/managers experience slightly more negative bias from subordinates, which increases when their style is more masculine.
- Men exhibit more task-oriented behaviors and therefore are more often perceived as leaders in leaderless situations.
- There are "no overall sex differences in leader effectiveness"; however, "employees were more satisfied with female leaders, but rated men as abler leaders" (p. 28).

Although women are as effective as men in the leader/manager role, they may experience discrimination because of perceptions that men are better and more capable leaders. To counteract this prejudice, women would do well to learn more about their own natural leadership style. Organizational advantages can be gleaned from their democratic style of leading and their encouragement of participation and collaboration.

Women and men need similar skills to successfully complete the career obstacle course—"persistence and guts," ambition, drive, hard work, self-confidence, competence, and commitment to career. Despite all of the similarities between successful men and women, perceptions of differences contribute to work environments that impose very different expectations for female and male leaders, according to Morrison, White, and Van Velsor (1987). These different expectations are responsible for the glass ceiling.

Jeruchim and Shapiro (1992) said, "An important reason that women have difficulty breaking the glass ceiling is the absence of role models to guide the way. Each woman must break new ground for herself" (p. 4). The next chapter explores the impact that the presence (and absence) of role models and mentors had on the women psychotherapists we interviewed.

# 6

## Mentors, Teachers, and Role Models

*Psychotherapy supervisors serve as the keepers of the faith and the mentors of the young.*
—Anne Alonso

While women are underrepresented in positions of leadership in the mental health professions, their numbers dominate as students of psychology and social work. Since 1980, women have continually and consistently outnumbered men as undergraduates in universities in the United States. Women comprise two-thirds of the total population of those majoring in psychology at all levels, undergraduate through graduate. Although these figures imply changes for the future, psychology is still a male-dominated field with 60 percent of psychologists being men. Of even greater impact is the fact that three-quarters of full-time graduate faculty in psychology are men, according to Jessica Kohout, Director of the Office of Demographic, Employment, and Educational Research for the American Psychological Association (Adler, 1991).

The growing number of women students entering the mental health field will need encouragement and guidance (as will the male students), in addition to knowledge and training, to become successful clinicians, researchers, educators, and administrators. Mentors are important sources of such support but historically have been less available to females than to their

male counterparts (Jeruchim and Shapiro, 1992). Various definitions agree that a *mentor* is a more experienced person who
promotes the professional growth of someone less experienced
(Bogat and Redner, 1985; Collins, 1983; Levinson, 1978; Zey,
1984). The mentor is typically in a position of power and can
teach the protégé the political workings of the organization so
that he or she can advance more quickly. The mentoring relationship itself includes "a stronger degree of identification between
mentor and protégé than in any other work relationship . . .
[and an] intensity of emotional involvement" (Jeruchim and
Shapiro, 1992, pp. 31–32).

The women in our sample suffered from an absence of
mentoring, especially by other women, or from limited access
to the seasoned members of the profession who might serve as
mentors. Authors Bogat and Redner (1985) say, "The literature that counsels young women to seek mentors ignores much
of the evidence that we have presented in this article. Male mentors are likely to select male protégés, and men are likely to hold
negative attitudes toward women's competencies. Furthermore,
the possibility of finding a female mentor is unlikely given that
female faculty are underrepresented in most departments and
are not typically in the appropriate career stage to be mentors.
In sum, the female student seeking a mentor may not be able
to acquire one" (p. 857).

This chapter provides guidelines about mentoring through
sharing the words of experienced psychotherapists about what
they learned from their mentors. We will look at models of mentoring that are more consistent with what we know about the
psychology of women and their developmental needs. We will
also identify the professional and personal qualities of effective
mentors.

The authors, Lourene and Judith, have been supervisors
of psychologists-in-training for a combined forty years. We have
noticed the following differences between our male and female
supervisees. The males have greater ease in proving their competence and in enhancing their marketability and visibility. Females are concerned about their competence and are more apt
to express it through sharing self-doubts and fears about being

effective with clients. They fear being unable to sell themselves to clients, referral sources, universities, and publishers. In an earlier publication about women psychotherapists who were in therapy, Judith identified low self-esteem as a central issue in motivating women to seek psychotherapy (Coché, 1984). The women also struggled with guilt about conflicts between their personal and professional personas. They worried that they needed to see themselves and to be perceived as tough and businesslike on the job, but gentle and loving at home. They sought strong female role models of the competent, self-confident, and accomplished psychotherapists they aspired to be.

We met when Lourene joined a supervision group of women psychologists that Judith was leading. When Lourene entered the group, she wanted to understand what it meant to be a *female* psychologist. She had had few female supervisors or instructors but enough clinical experience to know that she identified herself as a professional psychologist differently than her male colleagues. She was also aware that the clinical approach she felt most comfortable with and that seemed to be most effective with her clients was somehow different from what she had been modeled during her training. Lourene realized that she had translated the lessons of her male professors and supervisors into a framework that felt more appropriate for her. She wondered what other female psychologists were experiencing as they carved out their careers.

Lourene contacted Judith because of her reputation as a highly successful practitioner and an experienced supervisor. The women's supervision group was exactly the experience Lourene was seeking. During the three years the group met, members talked about their hopes and fears, many of which had never been expressed to male supervisors or in mixed-gender groups of colleagues. The group was a place where intuition and mutual caring were valued and encouraged. It is this respect for the "female experience" that many of the women psychotherapists who responded to our questionnaire found missing in their relationships with male mentors and valued most with their female mentors. Mentoring as it is traditionally practiced is hierarchical and, therefore, does not provide women with the collaborative style of relating that they prefer and through which they learn most effectively, according to Belenky and her coauthors (1986).

Following the third year of the group, Judith invited Lourene to help her analyze this supervision group experience and to publish and present the results of the analysis to professional groups. Judith also asked Lourene to fill a postdoctoral internship in group psychotherapy in her clinical practice. The internship included co-leadership of a women's therapy group. The former supervisor/supervisee relationship thus developed into a mentor/protégé relationship. Although Lourene was still the learner and Judith the teacher, the style of the relationship was collaborative. The next level of collaboration was the decision to be co-researchers when Lourene shared with Judith her idea for the project on the personal and professional identity of women psychotherapists that resulted in this book being written. Our relationship thus serves as an example of how women can mentor other women.

## Gender Differences in Mentoring Relationships

Joan Jeruchim and Pat Shapiro reported the results of their interviews with 106 women in their book, *Women, Mentors, and Success* (1992). The women they interviewed were successful in careers in law, accounting, medicine, academia, and corporate/business management. Of the 77 percent of their sample who had one or more mentors, 32 percent had male as well as female mentors (49 percent had male mentors only; 19 percent had female mentors only) (p. 210). The 32 percent who had male and female mentors described consistent differences between the relationships. Female mentors offered more support and role modeling while male mentors provided career advancement. The authors said, "Men tend to deny the intimacy involved in mentoring and emphasize the power/success piece while women do the opposite: they overlook the power piece and stress the support they received" (p. 9).

For those women in our sample who have had both female and male mentors, many found clear distinctions between the two emotional experiences. One woman said, "With males [mentors] what was valuable was learning to be more demanding of self and others. With females [mentors], generally bonding, learning by example, allowing myself to really *study* them — and their allowing me to do so." It appears to us that the dynamics with male mentors reflect a competitive stance while interactions with female mentors are more collaborative.

Another woman says, "I had two mentors, one of each sex. What was most valuable from my male mentor was his belief in me and his very verbal encouragement and 'greasing the skids' for me. My female mentor showed me the most by allowing me to see her and her work and her life up close. Both cared a great deal." She apparently benefited from the differences in how her mentors expressed interest in her development.

Although they valued both male and female mentors, some women felt their female mentors were also role models in a way that their male mentors could not be.

From a thirty-seven-year-old family therapist: "Until recently [my] mentors have been male and I've respected their knowledge and technique. Female mentors are more valuable to me, though, because we need to deal with the same socialization issues — gender inequality, juggling kids and career in a different way than men, and we speak the same language (for example, about care)."

An administrator, teacher, and mother of two said, "The people I considered mentors were women, especially one. This woman was a role model in many ways, as a family therapist, teacher, person of determination, courage, and ethics. The male mentors were valuable in what they had to teach, but their offerings were diluted by a belief system which saw women in stereotypic roles." A mentor needs to be an example for one to follow; a mentor needs to elicit respect from and have respect for the protégé.

The women describe many of the male mentors as having fulfilled the functions Daniel Levinson (1978) lists for the mentor: teacher, sponsor, host and guide, exemplar, and counselor who provides support and encouragement. But the most critical function is "to support and facilitate the *realization of the Dream*" (p. 98). The dream that Levinson refers to is the life plan developed by the young man between ages twenty-two and twenty-eight, his vision of career, life-style, goals, and ambitions. The dream is primarily defined by the occupation to which the young man aspires.

According to John Kronik, professor of Romance language studies and mentor to both men and women, prior to the 1970s, "the mentor of women had no dream to support; he had to instill one. The women I recall—even those that have gone on to brilliant careers—for the most part had no professional dream; they didn't even have what dreams were called in those days: motivation, ambition. Most often their recurring dreams were domestic; sometimes they suffered a confusion of dreams" (1990, p. 55).

Levinson acknowledges that women have greater difficulty than men in forming a dream: "Everything in society supports men having an occupational dream, but for a woman, there is still a quality of going into forbidden territory. . . . Though it's very important for men to marry and have a family, the big difference is that a man feels he is taking care of his family by working" (Brown, 1987). But as we have discussed earlier, women often worry that family and work are mutually exclusive.

According to Jeruchim and Shapiro, "In the 1950's and '60's most women . . . did not have dreams and visions of themselves as career or working women. In more recent years young women developed career dreams and goals, but these often conflicted with domestic roles" (1992, pp. 25–26). The majority of the diplomates and family therapists surveyed were in high school, college, and gradute school during those two decades. They reported that their "domestic roles" were *not* central to the timing of their careers. They achieved a very high level of career satisfaction, sometimes in spite of the absence of a consistent support system. That support system for men consisted of societal and familial expectations that they pursue their career plan and, in many cases, a mentor who paved the way for them.

Traditional "grooming" for higher positions has been denied women because it is based on homogeneity and favoritism (Haring-Hidore 1987). Those who serve as mentors choose protégés most like themselves and overlook or actively exclude newcomers who are different, such as women and minorities. Usually, it is the senior faculty, widely published researchers, and higher level administrators who have the status and visibility to be sought out as mentors. Because people in these positions are usually white men, the white male student, staff person, or junior faculty member will be taken under their wings most readily.

When women do have mentors, they are more often than not males, especially in male-dominated fields. Few professional women are in the position to mentor younger females. Also, women professionals may frequently be juggling career, child care, and homemaking, which gives them less time for mentoring responsibilities. The stress of maintaining and furthering their own careers in the male-dominated work world leaves them with limited energy. What energy they do have will often be spent on managing their family and personal lives. The separation of family and professional lives, and the woman's choice to maintain them both, is a challenge that many men do not have to face. Men's career identity closely defines their personal identity, and their social role as father and husband can be fulfilled by pursuing their career dream.

Unfortunately, this stress takes its toll on many women, both those who might mentor and those who are seeking mentors, as we hear in these words: "What was most valuable [in my male mentors] was their belief in my talents and their encouragement. What was least helpful (downright unhelpful) was their . . . inability to understand my insistence on working part-time while my children were small. I would have liked at least one women mentor to help me sort out the 'balancing' issues — but there wasn't anyone around who was balancing."

The following quote suggests another reason why female mentors are not more prevalent: "Most of my mentors were male. . . . [They] were in positions to teach me something (and did), positions which were uncommon among women in the 1960s. The few women I met in college and graduate school were so busy making their own careers work that they did not do any mentoring. In fact, women tend to perceive each other as equals, which often doesn't lead to a mentor-type relationship."

In women's propensity to value the *mutuality* of relationships, perhaps they overlook the value of experience and power
that they can offer as mentors. Jeruchim and Shapiro said,
"Women have not yet been socialized to bring this propensity
for relationships into the workplace. They have under-utilized
work relationships that can help them advance politically and
succeed personally" (1992, p. xiv). Other factors prevent women
from becoming mentors. "Interpersonal and internal prohibi-
tions, such as their competitive feelings about developing relationships with other women, prevent women from helping one
another. Women's political naivete about how mentoring can
benefit them (as the mentor) inhibits them from helping younger women move up" (p. 57). They have had limited exposure
to female mentors who could model the value to them of mentoring junior colleagues.

Many of the women respondents report having had few
or no mentors. How does this condition affect their professional
and personal identity? Levinson implies that the mentoring relationship is indispensable to one's career development. On the
other hand, Kronik (1990) says he did not have a mentor, and
he believes that one can attain success without a mentor, though
one will be handicapped. Without a mentor, a new professional
may be missing an important support system and an opportunity for valuable contacts.

Referring to their study of 106 successful women in various professions, Jeruchim and Shapiro report that "98% of the
women who had mentors said they were better off professionally, and 95% said they were better off personally because of
this mentoring relationship" (p. 132). The authors cite studies
that support that "women involved in mentoring relationships
have greater job success and satisfaction than women who do
not have a mentor" (p. 131).

Maggie Scarf (1980) concludes that the female learns to
appraise her own worth as a function of the appraisals given
by others — to value herself insofar as she is valued. Ruthellen
Josselson (1987) talks about the importance of having mentors
to help women identify their careers as being part of their sense
of self: "the experience of work will not become an anchoring

part of the sense of self unless there is external recognition by important others in the field" (pp. 176–177). For professional women without mentors, their careers, no matter how successful, may not serve as sources of self-esteem. Extrapolating from the several theories on female development that emphasize the importance of relationships in women's sense of self, we can conclude that many women derive personal meaning from their work in terms of how they care for others or relate to others through their work. Again quoting from Jeruchim and Shapiro, "No matter how prestigious their position, they told us that they couldn't feel successful unless they felt good about their personal relationships" (1992, p. 199). Women have, in fact, invented new models of mentoring where the traditional one has failed them.

## Models of Mentoring

The model of mentoring we have been examining thus far has been referred to as "grooming" and is the traditional model described by Daniel Levinson (1978). It is based on principles central to male adult development in which one's sense of self-worth is largely focused on success in one's chosen career. It is a hierarchical relationship in which the mentor guides the protégé to success. The relationship is developmental, characterized by four stages: initiation, cultivation, separation, and redefinition. These stages suggest a coming together and a moving apart, or a beginning, middle, and end of the mentoring relationship. These relationships tend to be homogeneous because mentors are likely to choose protégés similar to themselves, and that usually means a relationship between two men rather than between a man and a woman. This kind of mentoring is also based on favoritism because mentors will promote their protégés over others. Finally, relationships tend to be intense, especially in the final phase when protégés are ready to become colleagues and peers who can threaten their former mentors within the organizational hierachy. An example can be found in the words of two women from the sample: "One mentor [was] very supportive [and] taught me a lot clinically, but became irrationally hostile, apparently threatened that I, a woman, would be a professional." The second woman wrote, "The male [mentor] who was most important (my chief for almost twenty years) also prevented me from having a title (Director of Training) appropriate to my position because he wanted to keep that title along with his title of Head of Division."

When the mentor is not threatened by the protégé's accomplishments, however, movement up the career ladder is a sure and rapid process, a major advantage to being mentored.

### Networking

"Networking" is a model proposed by Swoboda and Millar (1986, p. 11) that, in contrast to grooming, "entails more flexible and mutually interdependent patterns of training, information sharing, and support." It is characterized by a sharing of the roles of mentor and protégé, a reciprocity between two or more people. Networking is based on mutual enhancement of career depending upon who is in a position to aid whom at particular points or in particular situations. Those who experience this style of mentoring are more likely to consider themselves colleagues or peers. These relationships are nonhierarchical and are available to all people, not just the chosen few. Other advantages include few relational problems because the support is mutual rather than one-way. Networking also promotes greater self-reliance because no one person is responsible for the other's advancement. There is less resentment by colleagues because of the absence of favoritism. And it is not subject to a mentor's career problems that can leave a protégé vulnerable by association. A disadvantage is that these relationships generally do not move women up the career ladder as rapidly as do grooming relationships.

An example of networking is suggested in this woman's words: "I had two male mentors and one female colleague who were influential. The men were role models for research, teaching, [and] for administration, while the female colleague was important to me, as I was to her, in sorting out family/professional role conflicts."

## Generative Leadership

"Generative leadership" was not proposed as a model of mentoring as such. Sagaria and Johnsrud (1988) described generative leadership as a substitute for women who do not have traditional mentors or do not serve as traditional mentors. "Generative leadership entails a collaborative effort in which leaders empower others to develop and accomplish goals" (p. 14). This leadership is not determined by position and authority but by one person being in a position to enable another to grow professionally. The generative aspect continues when the person assisted is then in a position to help others develop. The influence is linear—from person-to-person rather than from top to bottom as in grooming or interconnected, mutual, and ongoing like networking.

An advantage of generative leadership is that it tends to foster productivity, creativity, and a sense of self-esteem. Like networking, it emphasizes mutual empowerment among leaders and participants. It can be enacted in relationships that are less intense and of shorter duration than mentor-protégé. Although generativity is not gender-specific, as a leadership style it is quite compatible with the developmental theory of women that points out the centrality of relationships and caring as being fundamental to women's identity. It is a leadership model congruent with Carol Gilligan's findings about the importance to women of the values of caring and responsibility. A disadvantage of generative leadership, as of networking, is that its recipients may move more slowly up the career ladder.

Recognizing that women enter their careers at various points in the life cycle, or that they may stop and restart, or redefine their careers to adjust for parenting responsibilities, Jeruchim and Shapiro (1992) recommend a model for mentoring that accommodates a variety of supports. "As they progress through distinct developmental stages, women express their work identity differently in their twenties, thirties, and forties. So it's clear that women need a series of role models and mentors at different ages and at different times of their development, to help them formulate their work dreams, advance in their careers, and support them as professional women" (p. 2). They suggest that a woman have a male mentor to help her move up in her career, a female mentor to serve as a role model, and a series of "coaches," sponsors, peers, and bosses during periods when a mentor is not available. This "bits and pieces" type of mentoring encourages women to recognize multiple resources and to combine the connections and encouragement they receive from those who may not play the primary role that a mentor does. It is a method for compensating for the absence of traditional mentors for many women. The authors also advocate the use of "symbolic mentors," those whose work we read about but with whom we have no contact. Symbolic mentors can be dead or living, real or fictional, or mythical. Women need to be adaptive: "This is how mentoring is for most women today; they invent it in whatever form they can and use it whenever possible to benefit their career" (p. 131).

## Mentors of Women Psychotherapists

The majority of our experts' mentors were males, not at all surprising since most of the women in the sample were in training prior to the 1970s when most leaders in the field were male. Our experts report that these men were best equipped to help their protégés hone their clinical skills and learn about organizational politics. In addition, male mentors helped the women to challenge their lowered expectations of their own competence and thereby pushed them to grow professionally, to "be all that they could be." Male mentors may be better equipped to provide this boost to one's professional self-image because they have been the gatekeepers to the profession.

Women have valued these lessons from male mentors who encouraged them to be more demanding of themselves, to experience their power by taking on the challenge. But what they have valued most of all are the more personally supportive aspects of their relationships with mentors of both genders. While males may be more sought after for their approval, females are more sought after as role models, as we hear in the following two quotations.

A retired diplomate praised her male mentor: "The primary mentor in my life was male. He was a role model of the learned man — he taught me that I was worthwhile, that I was intelligent, and that I could make it in my chosen field. Without him I doubt I would have had the courage to go on to graduate school. I wouldn't trade him for anyone, male or female."

From a woman who graduated with an M.S.W. degree and had a majority of female professors and supervisors: "My most positive experience was the female mentors who not only became role models but also dear friends. Contact with these women supported my professonal strivings but also taught me how many people have to compromise their personal life to advance in their careers. It enabled me to decide that my career would always be secondary to my personal life."

What women found most valuable, independent of gender, were mentors who believed in them, gave them encouragement, and saw potential in them that they did not see in themselves. Table 6.1 shows how respondents rated what they valued most in their mentors.

Some respondents acknowledged clear differences in what they received from their male and female mentors; others felt that gender was not a factor in the quality of the mentoring relationship. "Female models are also important but [I'm] not sure

**Table 6.1. How Mentoring Helped.**

"Daniel Levinson, in *Seasons of a Man's Life,* highlights the importance of the mentoring relationship for males. Little is known about the importance of this relationship for females. Think of the mentors you have had and relate what was most valuable about those relationships for you. What was least valuable? Were your mentors males or females? Would you have preferred more mentors of your own gender? Why? Why not?"

|  | *Responses (%)* |
|---|---|
| "Counsel" function — provided moral suppoprt and encouragement | 52 |
| "Teacher/sponsor" function — provided skill development and career advancement | 23 |
| Combination of both "counsel" and "teacher/sponsor" functions | 25 |

[one] must have [a] female *mentor* in contrast to female support."
Another respondent said, "I think mentoring is different for
women. I wish I had had some female role models. My most
growthful relationships have been with younger female colleagues
who might call me their mentor and from whom I've learned
so much. I have grown in close relationship with men too. Intimacy and mutuality provide the climate for self-examination
and growth."

Some authors (Coché, 1984; Jeruchim and Shapiro, 1992)
believe that women need to learn from other women. Referring to women psychotherapists to whom she acted as therapist,
Judith Coché stated, "they need competent women mental health
professionals with whom to share their struggles and from whom
to learn" (p. 163). Speaking of women professionals in general,
Jeruchim and Shapiro noted, "we found that the male model
did not mesh with the contemporary woman's needs or with her
unique place in the work force. Women wished for a perspective on surviving and thriving in the predominantly male work
environment. They longed for a female role model to show them
how to combine their career and family responsibilities. In essence, they yearned for a broader, more eclectic perspective on
mentoring" (p. 192).

One woman reported learning similar lessons but in very
different ways from her mentors: "[I] had both male and female
mentors: both taught me to separate and *think*. ([The] female
taught me I could think and feel at the same time.) [The] male
taught me to plan [and] set priorities. [The] male got sexual when
I needed warmth. [There were] not enough effective females."

One of the things the women therapists want from their
female mentors is more recognition of special female qualities,
as the following three comments reveal: "With female mentors
[I would expect to get] validation of my way of seeing and be-
having and appreciation of more than one road to the same end
point."

"I would have preferred more females to solidify my understanding that the female voice makes a unique contribution."

"More women as mentors would have given me more per-
mission to use my own power."

Many of our more senior experts had male mentors almost exclusively. The following comments were made by respondents who were in their sixties.

"My mentors were all male. My age group had very few women to turn to. I am grateful to the men who helped me, but I believe women mentors would have been even more helpful because I often felt alone and like a trail blazer."

"My mentors, except for [one], were male — I needed more females, particularly older than me. I needed more validation for my warmth and for my intuitive mode of thinking — I also needed [role] models. (I created my own.)"

"My mentors were male rather than female. I would have preferred more mentors of my own gender. Male supervisors do not often understand the rapport between women, and some of their strategies violate such rapport."

## Harmful Effects of Mentoring

Mentoring relationships can also be detrimental to one's professional and personal growth. The "luck of the draw" is involved. Women may be especially vulnerable in negative mentoring experiences. Because of their lesser status and power in society, they can become overly dependent on a mentor (Jeruchim and Shapiro, 1992). Twenty-three percent of the "Woman as Therapist" respondents reported negative experiences involving both male and female mentors. In some cases, as we heard in an earlier quote, male mentors sexualized the relationship. One middle-aged diplomate stated, "All the mentors I had were male. They encouraged me to achieve at higher levels and to complete a Ph.D. . . . They also expect[ed] me to 'fuck' or 'fight'." Another respondent said, "Male mentors . . . were problematic because their professional 'lessons' were contaminated by strong sexual exploitive overtones, (I was very attractive as a graduate student and during my early career) and I had to constantly fend off advances and somehow still relate professionally."

Concerning the issue of the sexualization of the relationship between female students and older male mentors, we reflected on one meeting of the supervision group that Judith led and of which Lourene was a member. Judith was preparing a presentation on gender and supervision and was curious about the experiences of these six women. To everyone's amazement, all six women had felt victimized by sexual harassment during supervision or clinical training by an admired older male colleague. Even more amazingly, two of the women had never discussed their experiences with anyone because they feared recrimination. Although we cannot generalize from the experiences of six female psychologists who met in 1986 in Philadelphia, we can assume that sexual harassment within the field has been more frequent than most of us, male and female, would like to admit.

Negative experiences with female mentors were also reported and usually involved inadequate role modeling and relationships based on competition rather than collaboration. A young, unmarried diplomate reports, "I had one attempt with a female mentor. She was envious of my 'youth' and freedom. It wasn't a great experience."

A disinterested supervisor greatly disappointed this student: "I had one female supervisor who had a severely negative impact on me because she was more interested in courting male favor than in nurturing me."

Currently a professor herself, a woman shares her experience: "My first mentor in college was a disturbed female professor, the only female in the department. I had no female professors or mentors in graduate school, but two male mentors, who took good care of me. I would have been much better off with more access to more female mentors — many of the (male) lessons I've learned, I'm now trying to unlearn."

Her only female mentor, though less effective than her other mentors, was still significant for this expert: "I have had several important mentors — all but one was male. They were and are generous men who treated me with great respect — all at least thirty years older. I think the age difference helps a lot — more wisdom, less threat. The one woman is younger, less generous, more rivalrous, but still very important to me."

The label of mentor is not always officially acknowledged or formally bestowed. It is often through hindsight, or looking back on the relationship, that we identify someone as having been a mentor, thus individuals who influence our development may not be acknowledged as mentors if that influence is negative. Nor are the criteria to qualify as a mentor consistent. Mentors do not even need to be members of the same profession, since some of our women identified their fathers, mothers, husbands, and sisters as mentors because they provided support and encouragement in their careers. Levinson (1978), however, argues that while "the true mentor . . . serves as an analogue in adulthood of the 'good enough' parent for the child, . . . actual parents . . . are too closely tied to . . . preadult development . . . to be primary mentor figures" (p. 99). One woman in the sample points out similarities between mentors and parents: "Most successful women have had their fathers as their first mentor. [A] mentor, like a parent, provides initial training and support but also can be limiting when you want to take unknown paths or a dissimilar road on your own." Mentors, like parents, sometimes have trouble letting go.

We have heard from our experts how their mentors have been "good enough parents" as well as damaging influences. Our next profile is of a protégé of one of our profession's most respected mentors.

### The Torch Is in My Hands — Lori Gordon

Lori Gordon, Ph.D. (clinical psychology), is the creator of a psychoeducational model of working with couples called PAIRS. PAIRS was launched with the help of Virginia Satir in 1984, when a foundation was formed "to prevent marital breakdown." By 1992, PAIRS was being taught to over three hundred mental health professionals in Moscow, Paris, London, Scotland, Israel, and other locations. Lori Gordon wrote a book, *Love Knots,* which was published in 1990 and has been translated into five languages. Her upcoming book, *Road Map to Intimacy,* is scheduled for publication in 1993.

In studying a brilliant career such as Lori Gordon's, we wanted to know more about the mentoring she received from Virginia Satir and others. Lori has often mentioned that Satir was a role model and mentor, and she speaks of her when conducting workshops and training institutes for colleagues. In a telephone interview, Lori said, "Virginia Satir was the most powerful influence in my life. My father had a coronary when I was fifteen, and my mother died of cancer when I was sixteen. Virginia Satir became a surrogate parent for me, and I found the wisdom and inspiration that we all look for in a parent from her. Virginia Satir was a great synthesizer and an integrator."

Lori chose Virginia Satir as a mentor in a manner which she suggests to colleagues. She believes that women who are emerging from academic training would do well to explore postgraduate workshops. When women find someone whose work "resonates" or speaks to them, they should do everything they can to learn from this person. When she got to know Virginia Satir, this is exactly what Lori Gordon did. As a result, she reports that Satir "freed me to be myself—she was so natural." Lori says that it was inspiring to find a female leader who was profoundly insightful and knowledgeable, and who combined these qualities with exquisite nurturing ability and the gentleness that some women have. Although Lori has also had male mentors, she says that Virginia was outstanding in her generous ability to give to another person. "Virginia Satir strengthened your options for choosing. She suggested that you let go of things which no longer fit you at that time."

Lori Gordon also lists Daniel Casriel and George Bach as mentors who were important to her. "In academia, one mentor is perhaps sufficient. But in the real world, the opportunity to choose and to learn from a number of people that part of their work which is extraordinary, is valuable. To be free to explore, as in a menu—you can choose what appeals to you—you don't have to eat spinach if you don't like spinach."

One of Lori's contributions to her field is that she has developed a psychoeducational model for working with couples that enables them to improve communication skills within the framework of a normal, growing, constructive experience. In the language of family therapy, one might say of Lori's work with PAIRS that she has "reframed" an illness-based approach to couples work to an educational model that enables couples to feel refreshingly normal and proud of their interest in improving their relationship. She credits much of the reframing to Virginia Satir. She recounted an anecdote about Virginia leading a workshop in which she asked a participant, "Do you have a judging part?" The woman, obviously concerned that she would be viewed as judgmental, answered, "No." Virginia continued, "Do you have a deciding part?" "Oh yes," said the woman. "Choose that part," Virginia suggested. The woman's resistance faded. Lori remembered that Virginia Satir always enhanced self-esteem and self-worth through the manner in which she dealt with clients and colleagues.

In summary, Lori states, "I've had both male and female mentors. The female mentors gave me more hope as a woman to be successful. The males were encouraging, but the quality of help from a brilliant, nurturing, insightful woman (Virginia Satir) was most crucial."

Lori Gordon is a model of a woman who knew where to find the kind of mentoring she needed, pursued this mentoring diligently, and has gone on to contribute in her own right to a field begun by one of her mentors. Lori is now herself a mentor to hundreds of mental health professionals who wish to successfully intervene in troubled intimate relationships. Judith is reminded of an often-repeated statement by her late husband, Erich Coché: "The mark of a great teacher is to produce students who, in some way, surpass them." Virginia Satir has contributed greatly as a pioneer in the field of family therapy. Lori Gordon, as a protégé of Virginia Satir, has helped develop a new generation of family therapists who will, in turn, inspire others. Lori Gordon has integrated the work of Bach, Satir, and Casriel to produce her own original growth model. She summarizes, "It is a stunning experience for me to be leading this program [PAIRS] because, for so many years, I followed others, who have [now] died. Now it feels like the torch is in my hands."

## Guidelines for Identifying Effective Mentors

We have been making a case for the importance of having effective mentors to aid in the development of women's identities as profes-

sional mental health workers. We believe women can benefit
from the good counsel and support of male and female colleagues
who have preceded them as well as from those who are sharing
their journey. We believe that more women need to be available to provide mentoring to others. People do not earn the distinction of mentor on the basis of their years of experience or
their title but on the basis of the contribution they make to someone's professional development.

Levinson defines the mentor in terms of the functions he
or she serves for the protégé. Because this definition is more
task-oriented than relationship-oriented, it is probably a more
useful definition for male protégés than for female protégés.
Although we agree with Levinson, we prefer to expand the
definition by including the qualities of the relationship itself that
enhance the protégé's development. The following quotation
shows how even seemingly negative qualities can be instructive:
"Most valuable was a male therapist who was harsh and un-
bending — I learned from this adversity. It would have hurt less
if he had been loving — as was a colleague, female, ten years
older than me, who is still today my friend and mentor."

Personal qualities of the good mentor include a genuine
interest in the other, warmth, personableness, ability to listen,
willingness to set aside one's own agenda and biases. Kronik
(1990) says, "By tradition the mentor is protective, knowing,
trustworthy, caring. The mentor-protégé relationship includes
but goes well beyond teaching and advising. It stems from a
freely chosen mutual attraction that involves friendship and that
provides guidance and nurturing of a broadly professional sort
while bearing on the private dimension as well" (p. 53).

In choosing mentors, we believe women should look for
relationships in which they can thrive. Some women in our sample found male mentors who provided such a relationship and
female mentors who did not. "My mentors were males, but they
were very much in touch with the feminine (as defined by Western
society) component of themselves. Most valuable was the love
(that is, total acceptance, total attention to *who I was,* as a human being) that was given to me by my mentors. They vali-
dated my power, my intelligence, my gifts, and my capacities

to be an excellent therapist and psychologist. The females I trained under tended to be from the 'old school' of achieving women, bitterly competitive, not accepting of young female students. I was deeply saddened by this realization."

Can a male mentor empathize with the years of socialization and see the world through the lens of the female protégé? "It's extremely difficult to transplant yourself into the psyche of the other and dangerous to determine what might be best for someone whose gender sensitivities and obligations aren't the same as yours," (p. 56) said Kronik, a humanities professor, of his own experience in mentoring women. However, male psychotherapists, because of their training and experience in facilitating personal growth and understanding, may be better prepared to mentor women than are most male lawyers, business executives, and university professors.

## Male Mentors and Empowerment

How important to mentoring relationships is the issue of the power differential inherent in male-female relationships in our society? Can women learn to exercise the power to be leaders in their profession from the men who hold that power and may be reluctant to give it up? Can a man be a true role model for the woman who has chosen both career and family when he has not had to struggle with that choice himself, at least not with the amount of sacrifice and compromise that the woman has had to make? The power differential between mentor and protégé is already great; it is all the more magnified when a man mentors a woman. One woman in the sample stated that the advantage for her in having a male mentor was to learn the male point of view in this male-dominated society. As the women have told us, men have helped them face the challenge to be all that they can be.

Jeruchim and Shapiro (1992) warn, "Male mentors may currently be the link to power at the office, but for a woman to maintain her identity as a woman in a male-dominated environment, she must also rely on symbolic mentors or on female peers for support and role modeling" (p. xix). We believe it is dangerous, however, to see power as split along gender lines. Historically, that may be the case. But as women assume more leadership and their power is recognized, they will not be dependent upon men to empower them.

Female students do seem to be choosing more female mentors and are benefiting greatly in terms of professional rewards (Erkut and Mokrus, 1981). Women are looking for role models for balancing career and family and are finding them in ever-increasing numbers. In the words of Mary Ann Sagaria, "In contrast to men, in whose lives the career is central, women seek a balance between achievement and competence to be gained through meaningful work and the satisfaction and rewards of caring relationships with others. The concerns and values of women are embedded in the interdependence of human relationships" (1988, p. 6).

The mentor relationship can itself be an example of interdependence because both thrive through the relationship. Mentors have the satisfaction of being able to make a difference in the protégé's future, and they are challenged to set the best example for others to follow. Mentors' reputations are often enhanced by their protégés, who may quote the mentor in their research, dedicate books to them, or invite them to be speakers. A successful protégé can increase the visibility of the mentor among her/his own professional colleagues and build the image of the mentor as a good judge of potential for success. Since mentors usually are in their forties, fifties, or older, the relationship with a protégé provides an opportunity to evaluate their own career development and professional identity and to maximize what Erikson calls the developmental task of generativity.

What Anne Alonso (1985) said of the relationship between supervisor and trainee could be said of the mentor-protégé relationship: "The awesome privilege and enormous burden of parenting the young come to fruition in the moment when they set forth carrying our visions of the truth and our dreams into posterity. In the complex art of emotional healing that has developed in the last century, a group of professional parents have emerged who have labored to maintain old truths, to communicate them to the present generation, and to enlarge upon them for the future. Psychotherapy supervisors serve as the keepers of the faith, and the mentors of the young" (p. 3).

Finding mentors, or mentor-substitutes, is a challenging task for new professionals. As the young women professionals assume the ranks of their mentors, they can carry on the role of mentor to others and thus close the "mentoring gap" women mental health professionals have faced. As Jeruchim and Shapiro (1992) point out, women in all professions have this challenge in common: "Nevertheless *how* a woman learns a profession and gains a professional identity is the same for all professions. She learns by idealizing the mentor, identifying with him, and then internalizing the parts that fit for her" (p. 172).

# 7

# Rewards of the Endeavor

*People are puzzles, and I never tire of unraveling the*
*puzzles which a person, a couple, a family brings to me.*
— Anonymous

Our career choice is usually made at a time in life when our experience of the world has not yet ripened. For this reason, when some adults reach their forties, fifties, and sixties, earlier career choices have been outgrown. The women in our sample provide an exception. They rate job satisfaction throughout the decades of their life as very high. For some reason, these women do not tire of conducting psychotherapy, although psychotherapy, by their own admission, is a draining career. There must be inherent rewards in psychotherapy for our women that go beyond career advancement, personal satisfaction, and monetary gain. In this chapter, we will take a look at these rewards as discussed by our experts. We will then go on to cite future directions for the field.

The chapter has three sections. In the first section, we examine the rewards of the endeavor as reported to us by the women in our sample. In the second section, we discuss the uniquely good fit between the developmental needs of women and the career requirements of psychotherapy. In the third section, we discuss the implications of our findings for the future of the mental health professions for female psychotherapists.

**144**

## Is It Worth It?

The number of years required to develop the skill level of the psychotherapists in our sample is considerable. Many psychotherapists work for social service organizations and receive salaries that are much lower than those earned by women professionals with similar levels of training. When we consider the unique combination of a large investment in training and dedication, and the disproportionately modest financial benefits from the endeavor for many professionals, we realize that something special must be going on. Add to this mix that these are women of high levels of intelligence and motivation, that other career options were available to them, and that they chose to stay with this profession. Consider further that these women, after decades in this career, weigh their career satisfaction level as very high. Although their income level is moderate and on-the-job frustrations are moderate to high, these women nonetheless enjoy their work.

## Two Categories of Reward

In reviewing the varied responses of our experts to the "Woman as Therapist" questionnaire, we noted several explanations of the many rewards inherent in the career of psychotherapist. The rewards fall into two categories: the external rewards that society gives to women who choose this career and the internal rewards that contribute to their own sense of self and to continued personal and professional growth.

### External Rewards of the Endeavor

External rewards are as important to our women as they are to women in such professions as accounting, law, medicine, and business. A sense of increased accomplishment, status, and earning power provide important gains for women in this field. Self-sacrifice is in no way a motivator for success in our female psychotherapist. The four external rewards that are specific to psychotherapy, according to our experts, are financial stability, flexibility, recognition, and the variety of tasks.

*Financial Stability.* In 1992, well-trained and experienced independent practitioners in psychotherapy charged $80–$175 per hour for their services. They are in great demand. Simple arithmetic tells us that in a ten-hour week, our experts could earn between $800 and $1750 per week. The financial rewards of providing psychotherapeutic expertise enable a comfortable lifestyle for the independent practitioner. Psychotherapy has become a legitimate and respected way for men and women to earn a good living. Psychotherapy sends children to college; it sends families on vacation; it gives adults a sense of financial and personal freedom; it builds nest eggs; it funds retirements.

*A Highly Flexible Venture.* Our experts tell us that a career in psychotherapy enables them to be well-rounded individuals. In order to achieve self-esteem, our experts tell us that they need both career and personal satisfaction. The flexibility offered in terms of time commitments is a distinct advantage in the career of psychotherapy. A woman in her twenties can choose to work Saturdays and evenings in order to build a practice. An established, experienced psychotherapist can work during the daytime and leave her evenings and weekends available for personal relationships. Hours are flexible during the child-rearing years, enabling women to transport children from one place to another, to go on vacation, to write books, or to teach courses at the undergraduate or graduate level. Direct parenting is possible because of the potential flexibility of work hours. Independent practice, professional writing and teaching, and consultation are activities that work well with the multiple demands of women's various roles. The independent practice model makes it simpler for most female psychotherapists to integrate a variety of functions than if they were in a nine-to-five corporate career.

Because psychotherapy is as dependent on personal qualities and life experience as on expertise learned in graduate school and on-the-job, there is an advantage in having lived more of life. The greater the life experience of the psychotherapist, the easier it is for her to understand her clients, provide empathy, and connect solidly with the client or family in question. For this reason, taking a few years off in order to raise children, usually detrimental to women in such careers as law and business, is less of a disadvantage in psychotherapy. A woman who cuts back her psychotherapy career in order to spend more time in other ventures for personal and professional fulfillment is likely to have an easier time resuming a successful career than a woman in most other professions. In sum, flexibility is available both in terms of weekly time commitments and for periods of moratorium. Even during such a moratorium, the psychotherapist is gathering experiences that will eventually enhance her career.

*Well-Deserved Recognition.* Psychotherapists have risen in stature as the field has developed. As educated adults have come to understand that living successfully is in part dependent upon good interpersonal skills, individuals and families have turned more and more to psychotherapy as a way of improving poor habits and attitudes. In the 1960s, most people did not enter psychotherapy unless mental illness was the issue. Now, as we move into the 1990s, many seek therapeutic help to improve their lives. And, quite naturally, as more and more adults have turned to psychotherapy as a way to grow, the profession has risen in stature, particularly in the United States and Western Europe. Leaders in our field are considered leaders in the community as well. For this reason, the stature afforded to a female psychotherapist can be considerable. Our therapists report the pleasures of being recognized in their communities and their families as experts in relationships, as experts in being human, and as experts in living life well.

*A Variety of Tasks.* Women who complete an M.S.W. or a Ph.D. degree and go on to build careers in psychotherapy are women of above average and superior intelligence. They tend to get bored easily and need variety to keep themselves stimulated and growing. Their intellectual curiosity is high and is often not completely satisfied through personal challenges such as child rearing, volunteer work, and domestic activities.

One disadvantage of the practice of psychotherapy is the need to sit in one place hour after hour. The physical risks of sitting still for hours on end can lead to lower back pain, increased and unwanted weight, and intellectual fatigue from listening hour after hour. Although it is hard to get around the sedentary nature of the profession, our experts combine traditional professional services of a psychotherapeutic nature with a variety of related professional interests. Some women are administrators of colleges and universities, mental health centers, or independent practices. Some women author professional articles, contributions to newspapers and magazines, and books of a general or professional nature. Some women act as consultants to schools, businesses, and industry, while others combine an independent practice with a traditional hospital position. A myriad of possibilities exists for someone well trained in psychotherapy.

### Internal Rewards of the Endeavor

Our experts list those rewards that increase life fulfillment as their most important reason for choosing a career in psychotherapy. These internal rewards continue throughout the various phases in a woman's development and consistently offer personal and professional satisfaction. Three rewards that our experts describe are generativity, connectedness, and a sense of personal fulfillment.

*A Sense of Generativity. Generativity* refers to the human need to contribute to future generations and leave one's imprint on history. This need may be fulfilled through raising children, supervising protégés, or developing new ideas in one's field. Our experts described the tremendous satisfaction that they experienced from contributing to the welfare and growth in other people's lives. One family therapist echoes the words of others when she states, "By helping a couple resolve marital crises, I am certain that I am interceding positively in the marriages of future generations in that family." The direct practice of psychotherapy, whether done with an individual, family, or group, enables the psychotherapist to recognize her contribution to the lives of the people whom she serves. Although this activity is satisfying for all of our experts, it may be even more important for women who choose not to have children or who choose major friendships as a basis for intimate connections with others.

A second source of generativity within the professional community involves the related activities of role modeling, mentoring, and supervising younger women in the profession. Mentoring can be interpersonal, in the form of teaching others the craft of psychotherapy. Mentoring can also consist of putting one's experiences and ideas into print for younger colleagues to read.

*A Solid Connection with Others.* The pages of this book are filled with statements about the value of connectedness. Our experts find sustenance, both personal and professional, in connecting with the lives and families of their clients, their students, their trainees, and their colleagues. A spirit of cooperative venture is usually preferable to our experts, but where necessary, they will compete in order to solidly connect in ways that are satisfying and meaningful to them. They tell us that connection with others is worth competing for. One of our experts reported that she needed to compete vigorously with well-trained male and female colleagues to attain her current position as training director of a graduate-level project. Part of the reward she enjoys is the connectedness she has with her graduate students.

*A Sense of Personal Fulfillment.* The field of psychotherapy is intellectually and emotionally fascinating for those experts who choose to pursue it. Our experts tell us that it is both gratifying and personally humbling to be involved in the venture of psychotherapy. It is gratifying because our experts know that they are assisting others in areas of personal need. It is humbling because the psychotherapist is never able to take full credit for the changes that occur. The internal fulfillment offered by this combination of intellectual challenge and emotional gratification in seeing people grow is perhaps the greatest internal reward of a career in psychotherapy.

## Improving the Field for Women

As of 1992, the field of clinical psychology was still male-dominated. The gender tide is beginning to turn, and many senior
positions are now occupied by women. However, salaries and
seniority still seem disproportionate in relation to gender. How
can women achieve equal salaries? The answer is not simple.
In the last twenty years, special divisions have formed within
the American Psychological Association and the American Family Therapy Association to address gender-related professional
concerns. These task forces have continually raised awareness
of the inequality of the genders in salary dispensation, status
positions, and other related professional ventures.

## A Unique Match Between Gender and Career

When we examined the theories of female development in Chapter Two and the research on effective psychotherapy in Chapter Three, we found an excellent fit between female development, effective psychotherapy, and the attitudes and practices
of the women in our sample. We saw that relationships form
the basis of identity for many women. We realized that most
women adopt an ethic of responsibility and care, and that these
two variables are central in psychotherapy. When we take a further look at the substantial career satisfaction afforded by the
processes of mentoring and supervision, our original hypothe-
sis becomes even more useful.

### *Conceptual Foundations for the Reward of the Endeavor*

Jean Baker Miller shows us that growth occurs not through autonomy but through connection with others and that relationships form the basis of identity formation for many people and
most women.

Carol Gilligan tells us that many women practice and pass
on to others an ethic of responsibility and care. Responsibility
for themselves and others is part of their core belief system. Care
for their own welfare and that of others is an equally important

belief. Many women find it necessary to *concentrate* on putting themselves first. They discover themselves in danger of taking care of others before they take care of themselves. Female psychotherapists, on the other hand, are easily able to distinguish between self-sacrifice and professional care for others, as we have seen in Chapter Three. Our women tell us that sacrifice involves putting others' welfare ahead of our own but that professional healing in no way involves sacrificing one's own welfare.

Third, the importance of relationships evolves early in female development and remains strong throughout the life cycle. Psychotherapists act as a catalyst for personal and interpersonal change. They discuss the relationships in people's lives and help clients put their relationships together in ways that are meaningful to them.

## Central Variables in Effective Psychotherapy

Our sample tells us that empathy is one of two most highly valued variables in producing effective psychotherapy. This finding is supported by clinical research cited in Chapter Three. Certainly empathy is very close to relatedness, and relatedness is very close to the heart of women. Observational skills were also listed as crucial to effective psychotherapy by our experts. It occurs to us that women are excellent observers in part *because* they are so interested in the welfare of others. We tend to take a good look at what we care about the most. If we care about people and their lives the most, then we tend to be excellent observers of the human condition.

A third skill central in psychotherapy is the belief in human potential, which is remarkably close in concept to nurturing or mothering. Nurturing or mothering at its best is the practice of a belief in the potential of humans to grow and develop throughout life.

In sum, when we look at the research on effective psychotherapy, we find that the variables that make therapy effective are similar to the variables that make relationships effective: trust in the process of growth, honesty between individuals, and mutual caring between people who are interested in one another's development. This seems more than coincidence. Certainly, we can draw the conclusion that women find psychotherapy a good career choice in part because the work that they do entails skill in variables that are central to their own development.

## Implications for Teaching and Training

The results of our voyage into the lives and work of almost two hundred distinguished female psychotherapists in the United States warrant further attention. The results tell the history of the female struggle to overcome considerable odds through an undefeatable internal drive for accomplishment and excellence. The data tell us how the work of hundreds of women psychotherapists impacts their own lives and the lives of thousands of clients and colleagues whom they serve. The data also bear indications for the future of the profession of psychotherapy, and in particular, for teaching and training younger colleagues in the field. In this section, we explore implications for teaching, training, and the future of the field.

### The Centrality of Empathy

Our experts were unanimous in attesting to the centrality of the skill of empathy in the profession of psychotherapy. They echo the research of those clinicians who devised ways to measure empathy decades before our research was completed. Although our experts do not say that they were naturally gifted in being empathic, we assume that many of them needed little more than some extra training to use their expertise as active listeners. In those cases in which a clinician is not naturally empathic, training can be helpful. Our data underscore the necessity of teaching empathy where necessary, and of valuing it highly in those clinicians who have tuned the skill to a fine pitch.

In sum, the first implication for teaching and training from our research is that the field of psychotherapy needs to pay increased attention to the training and assessment of empathy in evaluating the skill of future generations of psychotherapists.

## The Role of Gender in Development

A second implication for teaching and training is the need to continue studying the effect of gender on human development, both from a theoretical and from a research perspective. Despite promising beginnings in the fields of adult male and female development, many of the concepts within theories about both genders are speculative in nature. Our data point to the need for increased research in career formation issues for both men and women. Specifically, it would be of value to study gender issues as they relate to male psychotherapists, and to go on to study gender as it relates to career development in professions such as law, medicine, and business.

Although good psychotherapy requires traits considered both typically masculine and typically feminine, the modeling process and developmental process are different enough for the two genders that teaching and training need to integrate skill building for both, but apply them differently to female psychotherapists than to male.

**Encouraging Diversity.** Most of the women in our sample were Caucasian women of middle years or older. These are the women who, for the most part, have risen to senior levels in the two highly competitive organizations that we sampled. There is a need for greater diversity among psychotherapists, a broader representation of minority populations. Scholarships to minority students, such as African Americans, Asians, Hispanics, and lesbian women, have encouraged diversity in the field.

Our study would have been more useful to the field had we had a greater diversity in respondents. The homogeneity in our sample is representative of the early development of the field of psychotherapy. We expect and hope that if a similar interview is conducted with women in the field in a quarter of a century that the sample will represent a more diverse and heterogeneous group of women.

## Women Need Leadership Skills

Our data indicate that more and more women are entering the field of professional mental health, and psychotherapy in particular. More and more women are rising to the top of their field, despite experiences with gender discrimination, sexual harassment, and unfair practices. Our data show that it is only a matter of time before the field of psychotherapy is unique in that women provide a greater portion of the service than men.

As the gender tables turn, females will continue to occupy more positions of leadership and power within the field. Although our female diplomates have been pioneers, and our female family therapists have already risen to positions of distinction, these examples provide only a small amount of data about the way women attain and maintain leadership positions. Many women are ambivalent about their own capacity to be leaders and bring a sense of personal and professional discomfort to the task of managing others.

It goes without saying that leadership training for the female psychotherapist is essential. A fourth implication for teaching and training is that women need increased training in leadership that is adapted to their own relational styles and values.

### Women Need Mentors

The final implication for teaching and training is that women need to seek out mentors with whom they can identify. There can be a series of different mentors at different points in the development of the professional, and mentors can be of both genders. Many of our experts suggest that male mentors were helpful in terms of career advancement and clinical skills, but that female mentors provided role modeling in a way that was not feasible from a male mentor. Many of our experts were extremely appreciative of male mentors from whom they learned a great deal and who offered them support when they really needed it. Many of our experts pointed out the necessity for increased female mentoring and longed for a second chance to receive mentoring from individuals of their own gender. Gender needs to be seriously considered as part of the mentoring process, and this variable is worthy of further clinical research, not only in the field of psychotherapy but in related professions as well.

## Advice for the Next Generation

As the new generation in the field of psychotherapy comes into its own, those of us who have been in the field have much to pass on to our daughters in the profession. A few points stand out as obstacles to avoid and overcome in the years that follow the publication of this book.

### Speak Up

The voices of women traditionally have been too soft and too passive. Theories and research in female development indicate that women have strong, competent voices with much to contribute in all fields of endeavor.

In Chapter Five, we noted examples of sexual harassment and gender discrimination perpetuated against women in our field. Although our colleagues are no more to blame for these incidents than are similar victims in other walks of life, changes in assertiveness should decrease these occurrences. Many colleagues said that they had been afraid to speak up because their jobs were in jeopardy or they were dependent on male superiors for grades and salaries. For this reason, they did not fight back against unfair treatment. It is essential that all of our colleagues who have been victims of discrimination or sexual harassment speak out honestly and openly to those who can help them. Not only is it essential for the well-being of our colleagues, it is necessary that those males in the field who have taken advantage of female students and colleagues learn that this will no longer be tolerated.

Speaking up has another advantage of modeling assertive and confident professional behavior for younger members in the field and for colleagues as well as setting examples for clients and family members. For these reasons, speak up.

### Don't Just Say It, Write It

One of the most powerful ways to advance in the field is to engage in professional writing. Many of our female colleagues, busy with the many demands of multifaceted roles as mothers, wives, and service-oriented professionals neglect to pursue professional writing. Even though more and more women are entering the field, a disproportionate number of the men produce professional writing and therefore advance in the field.

Editorial boards of journals need to be attuned to the importance of equality in representation. As female leadership in the field advances through the written word, the voices of women psychotherapists will become more and more evident. As recently as 1985, a proposal for a volume on women in psychotherapy was turned down by a major training group because it was believed that such a work would not be of sufficient interest to the membership. The only way to counter sexism is for women's voices to be heard, read, indexed, and recognized.

### Network Nationally and Internationally

Power in any field is distributed from the top down. Major conferences form the testing ground for future developments in a field. Once again, many women, limited in scope by the necessity to be home for children and domestic activities, neglect to put money and time aside to attend national and international conferences. Although local conferences are of value, they do not provide as much stimulation and do not set trends in the way that occurs when people from different parts of the country and world come together to share ideas and vision.

Women who work in institutions would do well to request professional compensation in terms of time and money for presentations given at national and international conferences. Attending meetings dealing with the future of the field and how to publish are of great value. It is through workshops and conferences such as these that many of our pioneers became known.

## What Is the Wisdom in *Powerful Wisdom*?

As we come to a close, we ask ourselves once again, what is so powerful about the wisdom of the woman therapist? We can conclude from our data that the wisdom of the female therapist is her skill in fostering human growth. Women therapists are achieving status, financial rewards, and recognition for being excellent mentors and teachers. The wisdom of women has always been the wisdom of personal and interpersonal nurturance. The additional power to control the future of the mental health profession is the recent achievement of women in this field.

The wisdom of the psychotherapist influences the lives of others. It helps people resolve crises. It motivates children in directions that will benefit them in the future. The wisdom of women has long consisted of strength in those qualities that enable personal and interpersonal growth. The anecdotes from distinguished female psychotherapists, set down in these pages, tell the story of this powerful wisdom as it has been applied in a professional adventure that influences the lives of all of us.

# The "Woman as Therapist" Questionnaire

A questionnaire developed by Lourene A. Nevels, Ph.D. and Judith M. Coché, Ph.D.

This questionnaire is a kind of "written interview"; therefore, some of the questions ask you to write out more lengthy responses. This kind of anecdotal information can provide much richer and more authentic material than could be gleaned from a standardized form. Other items ask you to simply fill in a blank or check the appropriate response among those listed. We feel that many of the questions are quite provocative and that you may take more than one sitting to complete the questionnaire.

If insufficient space is provided on the questionnaire for your responses, feel free to add an additional sheet of paper with further comments.

1. Your date of birth _____

2. Your gender   female _____        male _____

3. Your highest academic degree _____

4. Year degree was granted _____

5. The discipline in which your degree was granted

_____

6. Please check all work settings in which you have been employed since you received your highest academic degree.
   _____ a. private practice     _____ f. private agency
   _____ b. community mental     _____ g. teaching
          health     _____ h. research
   _____ c. hospital     _____ i. other (specify)
   _____ d. university     _____
   _____ e. business/industry     _____

7. What is (are) your current job title(s)? _____

8. During the past year, what percentage of your clients was female? _____

9. During your graduate training, what percentage of the students in your program was female? _____

10. What percentage of the faculty with whom you trained was female? _____

11. During your training and since, what percentage of your clinical supervisors has been female? _____

12. During your career as a psychologist, what percentage of your colleagues in your work settings has been female?

_____

13. How satisfied are you with your choice of a career in psychology?
    (please circle the appropriate number)

| very disappointed | | neutral | | very satisfied |
|---|---|---|---|---|
| 1 | 2 | 3 | 4 | 5 |

14. Are you currently single _____ married _____ divorced _____ widowed _____ ?

15. Do you have children? Yes _____ No _____

16. If so, what are their ages? _____

17. Please check the appropriate statement(s) below:

    _____ a. I adjusted my career to accommodate having
             children.

    _____ b. I began my career after my children were born.

    _____ c. I am planning to have children _____ more
             children _____ (check one) at a future point
             in my career.

    _____ d. I chose not to have children, in part, because of
             my career.

    _____ e. I am still not sure if I will have children.

18. How central in life planning was the expectation and experience of mothering in the *timing* of graduate school entrance, completion of degree, and professional involvement?

| not at all | | somewhat | | very central |
|---|---|---|---|---|
| 1 | 2 | 3 | 4 | 5 |

19. If you have children, what is there in your experience of parenting that is useful to you as a therapist? What do you give your children that is similar to what you give your clients?

20. As a daughter, what do you believe to be your mother's greatest impact on your development?

21. In your opinion, would your family be prouder of you if you married and parented successfully or if you achieved recognition as a psychologist? Might this reaction have been different if you had been male? How?

22. In the left-hand column below, list three values (for example, ambition, financial security, motivation to succeed, academic achievement, dedication to a higher goal) that were transmitted to you by your family of origin. In the right-hand

column, list those values from the left column that are central to your effectiveness as a therapist.

| Values | Central to therapy |
|--------|--------------------|

1.

2.

3.

23. The following have been cited as curative factors in the psychotherapy process. Please use the scale below to indicate how important each is to *your* effectiveness as a psychotherapist.

| not at all | | moderately important | | critical |
|------------|---|----------------------|---|----------|
| 1 | 2 | 3 | 4 | 5 |

_____ insight                       _____ research & theoretical
_____ observational skills          foundations
_____ empathy                       _____ cognitive acuity
_____ diagnostic skill              _____ capacity to nurture
_____ sense of humor                _____ belief in human potential
                                    _____ interpersonal skills

24. How has being a female affected your power as a therapist? How do the lessons you learned as a daughter and a sister, a wife and a mother, guide you in your work as a professional caregiver? How helpful were those lessons to you?

25. Daniel Levinson, in *Seasons of a Man's Life,* highlights the importance of mentoring relationships for males. Little is known about the importance of this relationship for females. Think of the mentors you have had and relate what was most valuable about those relationships for you. What was least valuable? Were your mentors males or females? Would you have preferred more mentors of your own gender? Why? Why not?

26. Are you aware of gender discrimination levied against you? If so, describe the worst incident. What action did you take in response? What action plan did you consider but not take?

27.  Recent advances in feminist psychotherapy have indicated
     that the formation and maintenance of satisfying human rela-
     tionships is central to the identity and life choices of female
     adults in all walks of life. How has the centrality of relation-
     ships affected your life decisions and sense of yourself?

28.  As a professional therapist, what do you believe to be *heal-
     ing* about human relationships? How do you use yourself
     in the therapeutic relationship to produce healing?

29.  How is professional caring different from the self-sacrifice
     that is sometimes associated with caring for others?

30.  What qualities or skills that you possess are most helpful
     to you in competing successfully in the highly competitive
     field of psychology?

31.  What have you learned about being in a committed love
     relationship with a friend or spouse that is useful to you
     as a therapist? What do you give to your friend/spouse that
     is similar to what you give to your clients?

32.  How does being a therapist get in the way of satisfying rela-
     tionships with husband, children, parents, friends?

33.  What have you learned from your relationships with your
     clients that you can use to enhance other important rela-
     tionships in your life?

# References

Adler, T. "Will Feminization Spell Decline for Field?" *American Psychological Association Monitor,* Oct. 1991, p. 12.

Alonso, A. *The Quiet Profession: Supervisors of Psychotherapy.* New York: Macmillan, 1985.

Barrett-Lennard, G. "Dimensions of Therapist Response as Causal Factors in Therapeutic Change." *Psychological Monographs,* 1962, *76*(43), 1–36.

Bateson, M. *Composing a Life.* New York: Plume, 1989.

Belenky, M. J., Clinchy, B. M., Goldberger, N. R., and Tarule, J. M. *Women's Ways of Knowing.* New York: Basic Books, 1986.

Bergin, A. E., and Lambert, M. J. "The Evaluation of Therapeutic Outcomes." In S. L. Garfield and A. E. Bergin (eds.), *Handbook of Psychotherapy and Behavior Change.* (2nd ed.) New York: Wiley, 1978.

Bernay, T. "Developing an Entrepreneurial Mind-set." *Psychotherapy in Private Practice,* 1988, *6,* 3–8.

Bogat, G., and Redner, R. "How Mentoring Affects the Professional Development of Women in Psychology." *Professional Psychology: Research and Practice,* 1985, *16,* 851–859.

Braiker, H. "The Secret of Psychological Stamina." *Working Woman,* Sept. 1986, pp. 129–155.

Brown, P. "Studying Seasons of a Woman's Life." *The New York Times,* Sept. 14, 1987, p. B17.

Carkhuff, R. R., and Berenson, B. G. *Beyond Counseling and Psychotherapy.* (2nd ed.) Troy, Mo.: Holt, Rinehart & Winston, 1977.

Coché, J. "Psychotherapy with Women Therapists." In F. Kaslow (ed.), *Psychotherapy with Psychotherapists.* New York: Haworth Press, 1984.

Coché, J. "Co-Therapy Supervision in Group Psychotherapy: Like Mother, Like Daughter." Comments prepared for the 47th conference of the American Group Psychotherapy Association, Boston, Feb. 1990.

Coché, J., and Coché, E. *Couples Group Psychotherapy.* New York: Brunner/Mazel, 1990.

Coché, J., and Coché, E. *Techniques in Couples Group Psychotherapy.* New York: Brunner/Mazel, 1990. Videotape.

Code, L. "Experience, Knowledge and Responsibility." In A. Garry and M. Pearsall (eds.), *Women, Knowledge and Reality.* Boston: Unwin Hyman, 1989.

Cohen, A., and Gutek, B. "Sex Differences in the Career Expectations of Members of Two APA Divisions." *American Psychologist,* 1991, *46,* 1292–1298.

Colby, A., and Damon, W. "Listening to a Different Voice: A Review of Gilligan's *In a Different Voice.*" In M. R. Walsh (ed.), *The Psychology of Women.* New Haven: Yale University Press, 1987.

Coleman, S., and Kaplan, J. "Their Family/Our Family: Who Wins? Who Loses?" *Journal of Psychotherapy and the Family,* 1987, *3,* 61–78.

Collins, N. *Professional Women and Their Mentors.* Englewood Cliffs, N.J.: Prentice-Hall, 1983.

Crits-Christoph, P. "The Efficacy of Brief Dynamic Psychotherapy: A Meta-Analysis." *American Journal of Psychiatry,* 1992, *149,* 151–158.

Davis, B. "Wife, Mother, Therapist, . . . Which Comes First?" *Psychotherapy in Private Practice,* 1984, *2,* 17–24.

DeAngelis, T. "Career Ladder or Obstacle Course?" *American Psychological Association Monitor*, Nov. 1991, p. 28.

Douvan, E. "The Role of Models in Women's Professional Development." *Psychology of Women Quarterly*, 1976, *1*, 5–20.

Eckardt, M. H. "Feminine Psychology Revisited: A Historical Perspective." *The American Journal of Psychoanalysis*, 1991, *51*(3), 235–244.

Eichenbaum, L., and Orbach, S. *Between Women*. New York: Penguin Books, 1987.

Eisenberg, N., and Lennon, R. "Sex Differences in Empathy and Related Capacities." *Psychological Bulletin*, 1983, *94*, 100–131.

Enns, C. Z. "The 'New' Relationship Models of Women's Identity: A Review and Critique for Counselors." *Journal of Counseling and Development*, 1991, *69*, 209–217.

Erikson, E. "Identity and the Life Cycle." (Originally published in 1959.) In H. Mischel and W. Mischel (eds.), *Readings in Personality*. Troy, Mo.: Holt, Rinehart & Winston, 1973.

Erkut, S., and Mokrus, J. "Professors as Models and Mentors for College Students." Working Paper 65. Wellesley, Mass.: Center for Research on Women, 1981.

Eysenck, H. "The Effects of Psychotherapy: An Evaluation." *Journal of Consulting Psychology*, 1952, *16*, 319–324.

Faludi, S. *Backlash: The Undeclared War Against American Women*. New York: Anchor Books, 1991.

Ferguson, A. "A Feminist Aspect Theory of the Self." In A. Garry and M. Pearsall (eds.), *Women, Knowledge and Reality*. Boston: Unwin Hyman, 1989.

Fiedler, F. "A Comparison of Therapeutic Relationships in Psychoanalytic, Nondirective, and Adlerian Therapy." *Journal of Consulting Psychology*, 1950a, *14*, 435–436.

Fiedler, F. "The Concept of an Ideal Therapeutic Relationship." *Journal of Consulting Psychology*, 1950b, *14*, 239–245.

Fiedler, F. "Factor Analysis of Psychoanalytic, Nondirective, and Adlerian Therapeutic Relationships." *Journal of Consulting Psychology*, 1951, *15*, 32–38.

Fish, J. M. *Placebo Therapy: A Practical Guide to Social Influence in Psychotherapy*. San Francisco: Jossey-Bass, 1973.

Frank, J. D. *Persuasion and Healing.* Baltimore, Md.: Johns Hopkins University Press, 1973.

Frank, J. D. "Therapeutic Components of Psychotherapy: A 25-Year Progress Report of Research." *Journal of Nervous and Mental Disease,* 1974, *159,* 325–342.

Freud, S. "The Dissolution of the Oedipus Complex." (Originally published in 1924.) In H. Mischel and W. Mischel (eds.), *Readings in Personality.* Troy, Mo.: Holt, Rinehart & Winston, 1973.

Friday, N. *My Mother/My Self.* New York: Dell, 1977.

Garfield, S. L., Prager, R. A., and Bergin, A. E. "Evaluation of Outcome and Psychotherapy." *Journal of Consulting and Clinical Psychology,* 1971, *37,* 307–313.

Gerson, K. "Briefcase, Baby or Both?" *Psychology Today,* 1986, *20,* 30–36.

Gilligan, C. "In a Different Voice: Women's Conceptions of the Self and of Morality." *Harvard Educational Review,* 1977, *47,* 481–517.

Gilligan, C. *In a Different Voice: Psychological Theory and Women's Development.* Cambridge, Mass.: Harvard University Press, 1982.

Gleason, N. A. "Daughters and Mothers: College Women Look at Their Relationships." *Work in Progress,* 17. Wellesley, Mass.: Stone Center Working Papers Series, 1985.

Hall, J. "On Explaining Gender Differences: The Case of Nonverbal Communication." In P. Shaver and C. Hendrick (eds.), *Review of Personality and Social Psychology,* 1987, *7,* 177–200.

Haring-Hidore, M. "Mentoring as a Career Enhancement Strategy for Women." *Journal of Counseling and Development,* 1987, *66,* 147–148.

Hymowitz, C., and Schellhardt, T. "The Glass Ceiling." *Wall Street Journal Special Report: The Corporate Woman,* 1986, Section 4, p. 1.

Jensen, J. P., Bergin, A. E., and Greaves, D. W. "The Meaning of Eclecticism." *Professional Psychology,* 1990, *21,* 124–130.

Jeruchim, J., and Shapiro, P. *Women, Mentors, and Success.* New York: Fawcett Columbine, 1992.

Jones, E., Krupnick, J., and Kerig, P. "Some Gender Effects in a Brief Psychotherapy." *Psychotherapy,* 1987, *24,* 336–352.

Jones, E., and Zoppel, C. "Impact of Client and Therapist Gender on Psychotherapy Process and Outcome." *Journal of Consulting and Clinical Psychology*, 1982, *50*, 259–272.

Jordan, J. V. "Empathy and Self Boundaries." *Work in Progress*, 16. Wellesley, Mass.: Stone Center Working Papers Series, 1984.

Jordan, J. V. "The Meaning of Mutuality." *Work in Progress*, 23. Wellesley, Mass.: Stone Center Working Papers Series, 1986.

Jordan, J. V. "Clarity in Connection: Empathic Knowing, Desire and Sexuality." *Work in Progress*, 29. Wellesley, Mass.: Stone Center Working Papers Series, 1987.

Jordan, J.V., and others. *Women's Growth in Connection*. New York: Guilford Press, 1991.

Josselson, R. "Ego Development in Adolescence." In J. Adelson (ed.), *Handbook of Adolescent Psychology*. New York: Wiley, 1980.

Josselson, R. *Finding Herself: Pathways to Identity Development in Women*. San Francisco: Jossey-Bass, 1987.

Jourard, S. *The Transparent Self*. (rev. ed.) New York: Van Nostrand Reinhold, 1971.

Kaplan, A. "Reflection on Gender and Psychotherapy." *Women and Therapy*, 1987, *67*(1–2), 11–24.

Kaplan, A., and Klein, R. "The Relational Self in Late Adolescent Women." *Work in Progress*, 17. Wellesley, Mass.: Stone Center Working Papers Series, 1985.

Kirshner, L., Genack, A., and Hauser, S. "Effects of Gender on Short-Term Psychotherapy." *Psychotherapy Theory, Research and Practice*, 1978, *15*, 158–167.

Kohlberg, L. *The Philosophy of Moral Development*. San Francisco: HarperCollins, 1981.

Kottler, J. *The Compleat Therapist*. San Francisco: Jossey-Bass, 1991.

Kronik, J. "On Men Mentoring Women Then and Now." *Profession 90*, 1990, pp. 52–57.

Lambert, M. J., Shapiro, D. A., and Bergin, A. E. "The Effects of Psychotherapy." In S. L. Garfield and A. E. Bergin (eds.), *Handbook of Psychotherapy and Behavior Change*. (3rd ed.) New York: Wiley, 1986.

Lerman, H. "From Freud to Feminist Personality Theory: Getting Here from There." In M. R. Walsh (ed.) *The Psychology of Women*. New Haven, Conn.: Yale University Press, 1987.

Lev-El, I. "The Entrepreneurial Woman Psychologist: Origins of the Species." *Psychotherapy in Private Practice*, 1983, *1*, 5–18.

Levinson, D. *Seasons of a Man's Life*. New York: Knopf, 1978.

Lott, B. "The Devaluation of Women's Competence." *Journal of Social Issues*, 1985, *41*, 43–60.

Luborsky, L., Crits-Christoph, P., Mintz, J., and Auerbach, A. "Predicting the Outcome of Psychotherapy." *Archives of General Psychiatry*, 1980, *37*, 471–481.

Maccoby, E. E. "Gender and Relationships, A Developmental Account." *American Psychologist*, 1990, *45*(4), 513–520.

McGoldrick, M. "On Reaching Mid-Career Without a Wife." *Family Therapy Networker*, 1987, *11*, 32–35, 38–39.

McGoldrick, M., Anderson, C., and Walsh, F. *Women in Families: A Framework for Family Therapists*. New York: W.W. Norton, 1989.

Marcia, J. E. "Development and Validation of Ego Identity Status." *Journal of Personality and Social Psychology*, 1966, *3*, 551–558.

Marcia, J. E. "Identity in Adolescence." In J. Adelson (ed.), *Handbook of Adolescent Psychology*. New York: Wiley, 1980.

Marecek, J., and Johnson, M. "Gender and the Process of Therapy." In A. Brodsky and R. Hare-Mustin (eds.), *Women and Psychotherapy: An Assessment of Research and Practice*. New York: Guilford Press, 1980.

Meltzoff, J., and Kornreich, M. *Research in Psychotherapy*. New York: Atherton, 1970.

Mendelsohn, J. "The View from Step Number 16." In C. Gilligan, N. P. Lyons, and T. J. Hanmer (eds.), *Making Connections*. Cambridge, Mass.: Harvard University Press, 1990.

Miller, J. *Toward a New Psychology of Women*. Boston: Beacon Press, 1976.

Miller, J. "The Development of Women's Sense of Self." Paper first presented at the Stone Center Dedication Conference, Wellesley, Mass., Oct. 1981.

Miller, J. "What Do We Mean by Relationships?" *Work in Progress*, 22. Wellesley, Mass.: Stone Center Working Papers Series, 1986.

Miller, J. "Connections, Disconnections and Violations." *Work in Progress,* 33. Wellesley, Mass.: Stone Center Working Papers Series, 1988.

Mintz, L., and O'Neill, J. "Gender Roles, Sex, and the Process of Psychotherapy: Many Questions and Few Answers." *Journal of Counseling and Development,* 1990, *68,* 381–387.

Mitchell, K., Bozarth, J., and Krauft, C. "A Reappraisal of the Therapeutic Effectiveness of Accurate Empathy, Nonpossessive Warmth and Genuineness." In A. Gurman and A. Razdin (eds.), *Effective Psychotherapy.* Elmsford, N.Y.: Pergamon Press, 1977.

Morrison, A., White, R., and Van Velsor, E. "Executive Women: Substance Plus Style." *Psychology Today,* 1987, *21,* 18–26.

Morrison, A., and Von Glinow, M. "Women and Minorities in Management." *American Psychologist,* 1990, *45,* 200–208.

Murray, H. A. *Explorations in Personality.* New York: Oxford University Press, 1938.

O'Connell, A., and Russo, N. *Models of Achievement: Reflections of Eminent Women in Psychology.* New York: Columbia University Press, 1983.

Orlinsky, D., and Howard, K. "Gender and Psychotherapeutic Outcome." In A. Brodsky and R. Hare-Mustin (eds.), *Women and Psychotherapy: An Assessment of Research and Practice.* New York: Guilford Press, 1980.

Pentony, P. *Models of Influence in Psychotherapy.* New York: Free Press, 1981.

Perry, W. G. *Forms of Intellectual and Ethical Development in the College Years.* Troy, Mo.: Holt, Rinehart & Winston, 1970.

Rogers, C. "The Valuing Process in the Mature Person." (Originally published in 1964.) In H. Mischel and W. Mischel (eds.), *Readings in Personality.* Troy, Mo.: Holt, Rinehart & Winston, 1973.

Sagaria, M. (ed.). *Empowering Women: Leadership Development Strategies on Campus.* San Francisco: Jossey-Bass, 1988.

Sagaria, M., and Johnsrud, L. "Generative Leadership." In M. Sagaria (ed.), *Empowering Women: Leadership Development Strategies on Campus.* San Francisco: Jossey-Bass, 1988.

Sandel, S. "Moving into Management." *The Arts in Psychotherapy,* 1987, *14,* 109–112.

Sandler, B. "The Campus Climate Revisited: Chilly for Women Faculty, Administrators, and Graduate Students." Project on the Status and Education of Women. Washington, D.C.: Association of American Colleges, 1986.

Scarborough, E., and Furumoto, L. *Untold Lives: The First Generation of American Women Psychologists.* New York: Columbia University Press, 1987.

Scarf, M. *Unfinished Business — Pressure Points in the Lives of Women.* New York: Ballantine Books, 1980.

Sloane, R., and Staples, F. "Psychotherapy Versus Behavior Therapy: Implications for Future Psychotherapy Research." In J. Williams and R. Spitzer (eds.), *Psychotherapy Research: Where Are We and Where Should We Go?* New York: Guilford Press, 1984.

Smith, M. L., and Glass, G. V. "Meta-Analysis of Psychotherapy Outcome Studies." *American Psychologist,* 1977, *32,* 752–760.

Smith, M. L., Glass, G. V., and Miller, T. I. *The Benefits of Psychotherapy.* Baltimore, Md.: Johns Hopkins University Press, 1980.

Stiver, I. F. "The Meaning of Care: Reframing Treatment Models." *Work in Progress,* 20. Wellesley, Mass.: Stone Center Working Paper Series, 1985.

Strupp, H. "On the Basic Ingredients of Psychotherapy." *Journal of Consulting and Clinical Psychology,* 1973, *41,* 1–8.

Surrey, J. "Self-in-Relation: A Theory of Women's Development." *Work in Progress,* 13. Wellesley, Mass.: Stone Center Working Papers Series, 1985.

Swoboda, M., and Millar, S. "Networking Mentoring: Career Strategy of Women in Academic Administration." *Journal of National Association of Women Deans, Administrators, and Counselors,* 1986, *49,* 8–13.

Symonds, A. "Gender Issues and Horney Theory." *The American Journal of Psychoanalysis,* 1991, *51*(3), 301–312.

Truax, C., and Mitchell, K. "Research on Certain Therapists' Interpersonal Skills in Relation to Process and Outcome." In A. E. Bergen and S. L. Garfield (eds.), *Handbook of Psychotherapy and Behavior Change.* New York: Wiley, 1971.

Walsh, M. R. *The Psychology of Women.* New Haven, Conn.: Yale University Press, 1991.

Walters, M., Carter, B., Papp, P., and Silverstein, O. *The Invisible Web: Gender Patterns in Family Relationships.* New York: Guilford Press, 1988.

Zey, M. *The Mentor Connection.* Homewood, Ill.: Business One Irwin, 1984.

# Index